BRITAIN IN OLD PHO

LADYWOOD

NORMAN BARTLAM

SUTTON PUBLISHING LIMITED

Sutton Publishing Limited
Phoenix Mill · Thrupp · Stroud
Gloucestershire · GL5 2BU

First published 1999

Title page photograph: The author's grandparents in St Mark's Street, with some of the family, early 1930s. Left to right: Doreen, Mary, Kathleen, Edna and Nora, aged eight, who was to become the author's mother. Standing in front is Joan. The babe in arms is David and the lad on the scooter is John.

British Library Cataloguing in Publication Data
A catalogue record for this book is available from the British Library.

ISBN 0-7509-2071-8

Typeset in 10.5/13.5 Photina.
Typesetting and origination by
Sutton Publishing Limited.
Printed in Great Britain by
Ebenezer Baylis, Worcester.

To Our Nan and the hundreds like her

St John's Church, Ladywood: The Arts and Education Development Project

St John's Church, built 1852–4, is a powerful symbol of continuity and Christian faith throughout the changing times recorded in this fascinating book.

The exterior of the church building was restored in 1998/9 with the support of the Heritage Lottery Fund. Inside, it offers great potential with its fine space and acoustics. Plans are underway for an Arts and Education programme to incorporate performances of music, drama and dance, exhibitions of art and religious education. St John's will continue to be the centre of Anglican worship in Ladywood. In partnership with the community – including the local Buddhists – it will become a creative meeting-place welcoming all-comers: a modern expression of the spirit of Ladywood for 2000.

Large-scale funds are required to modernise the interior for such purposes, through improvements to lighting, seating, heating and catering.

St John's appreciates Norman Bartlam's generosity in donating to St John's a percentage of his royalties from the sale of this book.

Appeal Director: the Revd Richard Tetlow, St John's Vicarage, Darnley Road, Ladywood, Birmingham, B16 8TF

CONTENTS

	Map	4
	Introduction	5
1.	Developing Ladywood	7
2.	Work	49
3.	Leisure	83
4.	Rebuilding Ladywood	131
	Acknowledgements	159
	Index of Street Names	160

Awaiting bathtime!

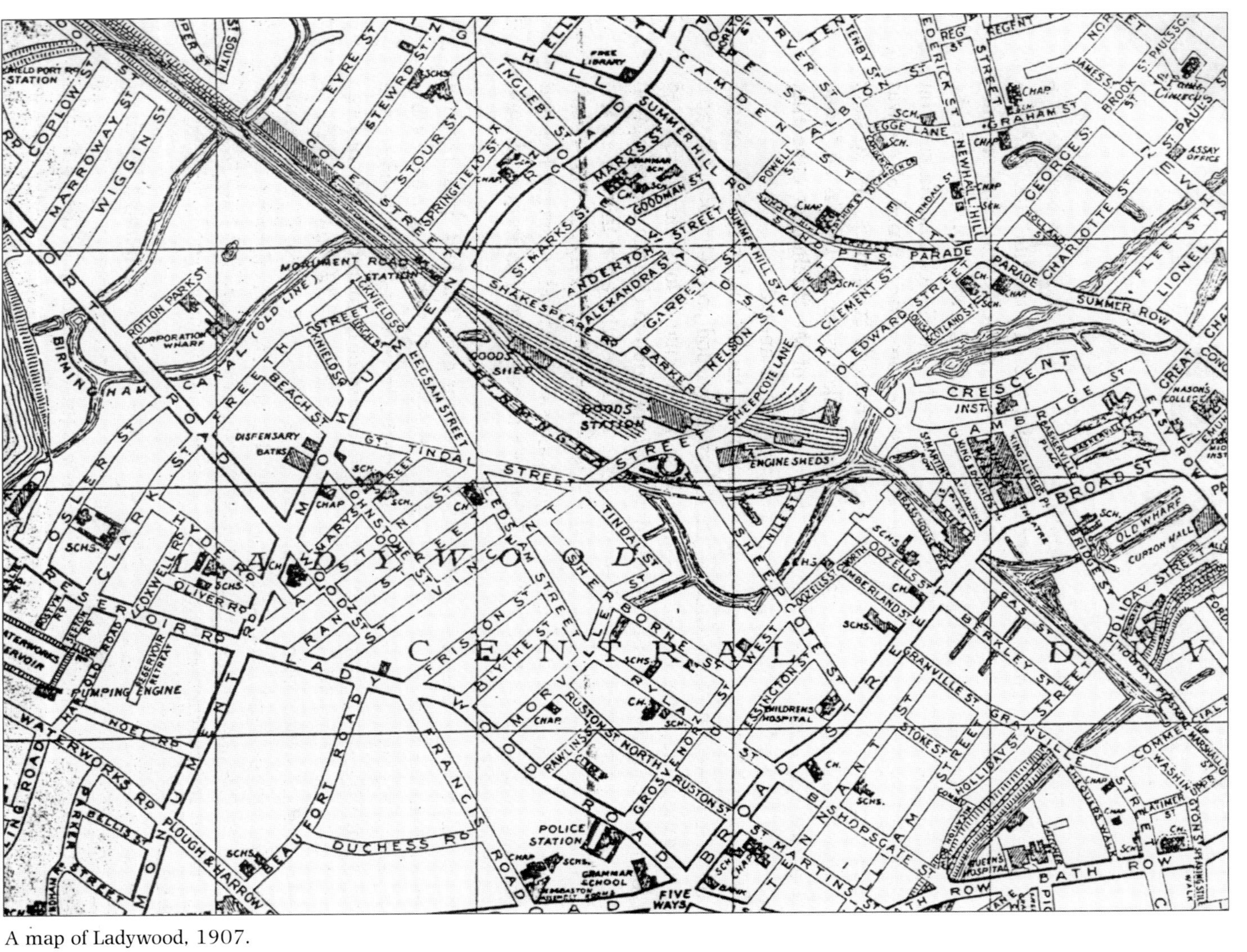

A map of Ladywood, 1907.

INTRODUCTION

Rolling mills rather than rolling hills are things associated with Ladywood, a district of Birmingham which helped to give the city the title 'the city of a thousand trades'. The name Ladywood, though, suggests that this was once an area of rolling green countryside. Names such as Spring Hill, Brookfields, Sandpits and Winson Green are the evidence we need. The Plough and Harrow inn built in 1704 took its name from the green pastures around it. Broad Street was once Pig Lane and the deer logo of Mitchell and Butler's brewery is said to have come from the deer which Mr Butler saw as he walked from the Crown on Broad Street across the fields of Ladywood to the brewery of Mr Mitchell at Cape Hill. Perrott's Folly was a likely vantage point to observe these animals.

The land on which St John's Church stands was in the 1380s land which formed part of the endowment of the Guild of the Cross. Ladywood probably took its name from this group and today there is a Guild Close. An avenue of lofty elms connected a large house, Ladywood House, with Ladywood Lane and the Cottage of Content off Sheepcote Street. By 1810, when Kempson drew a map of the area, there were few roads. Ladywood Lane ran from the toll gates at Five Ways alongside Pest Heath where stories of a plague pit originated. The lane swung round to Spring Hill and Summerhill. Nearby stood Roach Pool which was to be enlarged to form Edgbaston Reservoir to help feed the canals.

The canals were to change the face of Ladywood for ever. The first canal reached Ladywood from the Black Country in 1769 and immediately the cost of transporting goods, and bringing in raw materials, was drastically reduced. Within fifty years factories lined the canals from Ladywood to the centre of Birmingham where large wharves had been established off Oozells Street and Paradise. Landowners such as the King Edward's Foundation sold off land for factories and housing. The Ryland family laid out the land near Five Ways. By the mid-1840s Ladywood began to develop in two separate parts, around Great Tindal Street and around King Edward's Road, where the railways began to rival canals and extensive goods yards were established.

The growth of the population led to the establishment of St John's Church in 1852. The uncontrolled growth of working-class housing began to spiral out of control. The housing demolition of the 1960s was the direct result of the unplanned build 'em quick developments in the years just before the turn of the century. Life in those years was as hard and this continued to the 1960s. Lillian Carleton, who was born in 1914, recalls in her unpublished diary: 'having a pretty hard life, we were all very poor. When we had a boiled egg for breakfast we could only have one between two, but we survived.' Such poverty was by no means uncommon among the people of Ladywood. Most of the terraced back-to-back houses had no bathroom, no hot water, and a toilet down the yard which was shared by many families. The yard also contained the brewhouse, where a dolly tub was used for washing clothes. A tin bath hung from the wall for bathing youngsters while adults often used the public baths. In these areas everyone seemed to help each other and there was a great community spirit. The phrase about being able to go out and leave your front door open rings true – not that there was much for anyone to steal!

Ladywood people worked hard, in huge factories such as Belliss and Morcom and Docker Brothers, and in hundreds of small back-street concerns which kept the country running. An important chapter in this book looks at people at work.

If people worked hard then they certainly played hard as well. A chapter about leisure time contains a range of photographs that prove leisure time was well earned and not to be wasted. For many people this meant the corner pub. Pubs were as important as the corner shop. Most had their own darts or football teams. Ladywood had more than its share of 'flea pits' and was lucky enough to have the ice rink at Summerhill and the best dance hall in the city, the Palais de Danse.

By the late 1940s Ladywood had decayed to such an extent that a comprehensive redevelopment package was drawn up for slum clearance, continuing a process begun by enemy action in the war. This redevelopment scheme was successful in separating housing from industry and in creating valuable open space, but the redevelopment was fragmented and took too long, leading Norman Power, vicar of St John's, to call the people of the area 'The Forgotten People'. The old shopping areas such as Monument Road were torn down and the community was broken up. The new tower blocks, Power argued, created unequal and dispersed communities in which people lived in square boxes cut off from friends and neighbours. This, he said, was because the government failed to consider the value and place of the community. The new housing cut off people from each other and Ladywood Middleway cut the remains of Ladywood in two.

In recent years the council and community have been trying to put right the mistakes of the 1960s, and community and residents' groups have worked with the council on expensive regeneration projects to put the heart back into Ladywood, and to create a community to take Ladywood into the new millennium with renewed confidence and optimism.

CHAPTER ONE

DEVELOPING LADYWOOD

A typical mid-1960s courtyard scene.

Perrott's Folly was built by a wealthy local landowner, John Perrott, in 1758, making it the oldest surviving building in Ladywood. The reason it was built is not clear, but the view from the top certainly is, or was, clear for all to see! It has been suggested that Mr Perrott built it to watch for deer jumping across his fields; other suggestions are that he could keep watch from the top on his lady friends or see his estate at Belbroughton, although the Clent Hills may have obscured the view! It may have been the country's first vertical keep fit centre, because you needed to climb 139 steps to reach the top of the 97 ft high building! When Perrott died in 1851 the entire estate was sold to penmaker Joseph Gillott. His Nibs later sold it, and in 1884 it became one of the world's first weather recording and forecasting stations. Much of the early work was done by Abraham Follett Osler. Sadly it closed after ninety-five years of service. The highest temperature recorded was 94° F in the shade, the lowest 24° of frost. The view on the left was taken in about 1932, and the one below in about 1967.

The Plough and Harrow on the Hagley Road has been an important landmark since 1704 when local craftsmen built a wayside inn with extensive stabling. The name reflected the surroundings at the time. The building was pulled down and a larger one built on the same site in 1832, but part of the stables and part of the original vaulted cellars still remain. Today it is a popular hotel with forty-four bedrooms. There is no date on this postcard, but the motor buses which ran from the city centre to the Kings Head were introduced along the Hagley Road in 1903.

Note the squire and his helper standing at the road junction. Clearly one of them has got some work to do. Notable citizens began to make the inn a meeting place for social gatherings and dinners. The High Sheriff of Warwickshire resided there for many years during the Assizes, and Cardinal Newman arranged luncheons for guests visiting the Oratory.

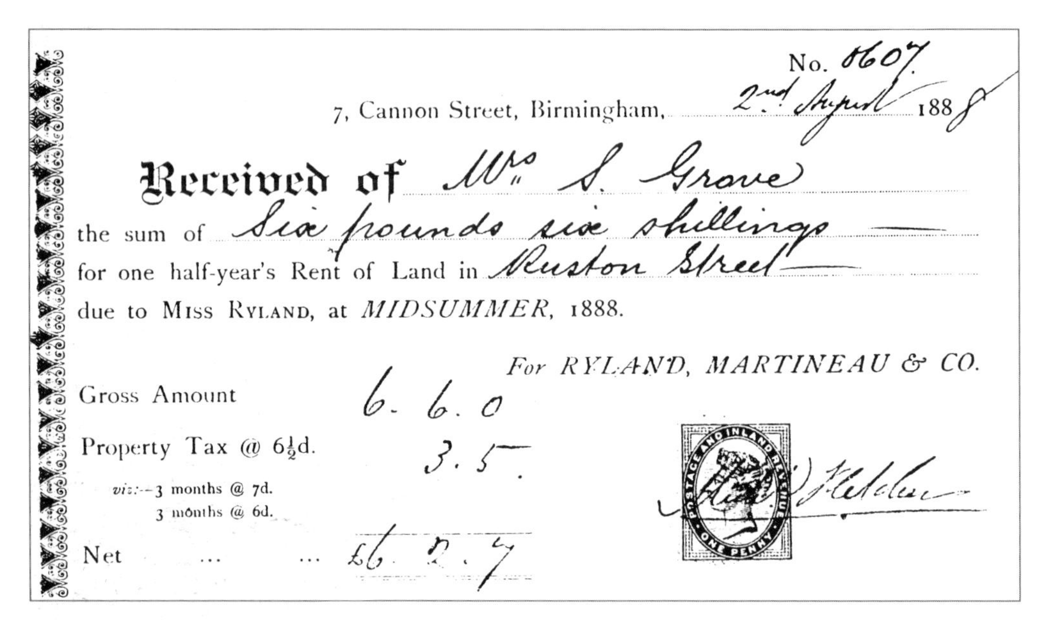

No. 0607.

7, Cannon Street, Birmingham, 2nd August 1888

Received of Mrs S. Grove

the sum of Six pounds six shillings

for one half-year's Rent of Land in Ruston Street

due to Miss Ryland, at *MIDSUMMER*, 1888.

For RYLAND, MARTINEAU & CO.

Gross Amount 6. 6. 0

Property Tax @ 6½d. 3. 5

viz:—3 months @ 7d.
3 months @ 6d.

Net £6. 2. 7

POSTAGE AND INLAND REVENUE
ONE PENNY

The open land was carved up and sold for building. That near to Broad Street belonged to the Ryland family. One half year's rent of land in 1888 cost £6 *2s 7d*. Ruston Street was a name given by the Rylands to the thoroughfare to mark a family name for posterity. Ruston was the maiden name of John Ryland's wife Martha.

On the fringes of Ladywood there were some high-class houses; many of them still stand today. This view of Monument Road is from a postcard which was posted in 1932. The written text on the back informed the reader that the writer had arrived back safely in London. She met Nellie at the station. Unfortunately an old man on the train was said to have been 'very talkative and he took snuff all the way'. At this time the average Ladywood child would probably never have been on a train and certainly would never have been to London.

Beaufort Road, 1908. Like many nearby roads it is named after the land-owning Calthorpe family. The fourth Lord Calthorpe, Frederick, married Lady Charlotte Sophia Somerset, daughter of the sixth Duke of Beaufort, hence Somerset, Charlotte and Beaufort roads.

Duchess Road is named in honour of the Duke of Beaufort's wife. At the turn of the century author J.R.R. Tolkien lived at no. 37. The nearby folly and waterworks tower are thought to be the towers which inspired Minas Morgul and Minas Tirith, the 'Towers of Gondor' after which the second volume of *The Lord of the Rings* is named.

Monument Road, *c.* 1905. Elsie Humphries, now Mrs Rafferty, recalls her mother describing the captivating views across Ladywood. 'At that time there were wide open spaces and you could see as far as the prison at Winson Green and only fields of green separated Ladywood from it.'

Another view of Monument Road, looking towards St John's Church. The road got its name from the adjacent Perrott's Folly, known more commonly as the Monument.

A slightly closer view of the stretch of Monument Road, with the church appearing from the buildings on Darnley Road. The lamppost is at the junction of Oliver Road. The large building fading into the distance is the imposing baths. The shops here included an ironmonger, a laundry, confectioner, bootmaker and a dressmaker. The large sign on the upper wall by the carriage indicates the building was a parcel receiving office for the Midland & North Western Railway Co. Today it is the site of the Birmingham Hospital Saturday Fund headquarters.

The small shopping streets like the one above gradually found competition from shopping parades which grew up along the roads. This view from 1923 shows Five Ways with Broad Street going down towards the city centre. Many of the shops here moved into Auchinleck Shopping Centre when it opened in 1970. The centre was named after Field Marshal Sir Claude Auchinleck, a former Supreme Commander of the armed forces in India and Pakistan. His only connection with the area appears to be that he was chairman of the company which built the centre. Wilton's clothes shop was the last of the original shops in it to close down; it closed for the final time in 1992, having been on Broad Street since at least 1886. Intriguingly the message on this postcard reads: 'In here for the day seeing about delivery of a dozen bodies with Alf.'!

Ryland Street was one of those that linked Broad Street with central Ladywood, and so attracted many passers-by who used the shops. In this view, taken in August 1961, J.A. Turtle the newsagent was clearly aware of the importance of advertising. Large advertisements include those for *Radio Times* and Wills's Woodbines. Next door has adverts for Typhoo tea and Senior Service cigarettes. Stowar's, in the middle, was a cooked meats shop.

Advertising is again prominent on this undated picture at the junction of Ryland Street and Grosvenor Street West. Joe's Café advertised itself with these messages: 'Cleanliness and Civility our Motto' and 'Stop for a good cup of tea'. Other prominent signs advertised hot and cold sandwiches. On the wall joining Grosvenor Street West there is a large Wall's Lime Split advert. The milk float coming up Ryland Street bears the registration number VOM 703. The building on the immediate right belongs to the Birmingham Guild.

Standing proudly outside this shop at the corner of Ruston Street and Morville Street in 1909 are the staff of the Co-op. The Ruston Street road sign can be seen high up on the wall on the right. The Great Francis Street address was that of the head office in Duddeston. A fore-runner of the Co-op as we know it was set up in Ladywood in the 1860s; the chairman was George Dixon.

Nos 126–3 Ladywood Road, late 1974. Two of them bear the 'Danger Demolition' signs. Many similar houses still exist in the Stirling Road area. What dates this picture are the cars, which include a Ford Anglia.

At the 'top end' of Monument Road at the junction with Parker Street stood Caves, which sold all sorts of furniture, seen here in the early 1960s. At one time another branch traded on the opposite side of the road. Myra Curley recalls: 'We used to walk along there to look at the bright lights in the window. It was a pleasure just to spend time window shopping! It really annoys me to see how this corner has deteriorated.'

This is the premises of the 'coffin makers and funeral carriage proprietors' on Ladywood Road. Thomas Furber's was established in 1868. The photograph was taken in January 1975 shortly before the building went to the great building site in the sky. In days gone by Furber's horses and funeral carriages were a well-known local sight.

Alston Street, April 1974. Over the entry on the right there is a stone which bears the inscription 'Victoria Buildings'. Alston Street is another which gets its name from the local landowner's family. Louisa Ryland, who was John Ryland's grand-daughter, loved Henry Smith, but he married someone else. Louisa, however, never forgot him and is said to have left her fortune in 1889 to Henry's son, on the condition that he adopted her surname – and so he became Charles Alston Smith-Ryland.

Chamberlain Gardens with Monument Road in the background.

St John's Church seems strangely penned in by surrounding buildings on this view from 1961. The shops on both sides have now gone. The greengrocer's shop was run at the time by Norman Downes. The zebra crossing indicates how busy it was on this stretch of road. The photographer was standing on the corner of Hyde Road.

The same view today. The car park of the Birmingham Hospital Saturday Fund stands on the site of the greengrocer's. Hyde Road has disappeared and a new Oratory School has been built across it. The grass area is the edge of the school car park. Scaffolding had just been removed from the church following the successful restoration appeal.

Local historians at the Oratory School in 1995 discovered where Hyde Road once ran and these two pupils, David Nugent and Stacey Devlin, found out that they were sitting where the living rooms of 5 and 7 Hyde Road were once located.

Hyde Road, January 1961. This was taken from outside the old Oratory School looking towards Clark Street and Coxwell Road. The Ansells sign is on the wall of the off licence, known locally as an 'outdoor'. The Hyde Arms is at the next junction.

Above: A family group in Reservoir Avenue off Osler Street, 1919. It shows a group posing in their Sunday best. The gentleman of the house is Tom Hexley, a building worker, and he was photographed with his wife May and children Kitty, Esther, Tom, Hilda and James. Tom, who is sitting patiently on his mother's knee, is now 'about eighty years old', according to Ken Strangward who loaned the photo. Tom is his grandfather.

Left: Osler Street, November 1965. The lad by the washing may well be celebrating West Brom's 6–2 victory over Fulham in Division One! This was Court no. 16 near the junction of Reservoir Road.

Jimmy Leaver's shop on Icknield Port Road, *c.* 1928. The lettering in the window reads 'J. Leaver English & Foreign Fruiterer'.

Jimmy Leaver with Eliza and three other folk, two of whom were from the Beet family. They are pictured behind the shop at the rear of 315 Icknield Port Road, which was near the Freeth Arms.

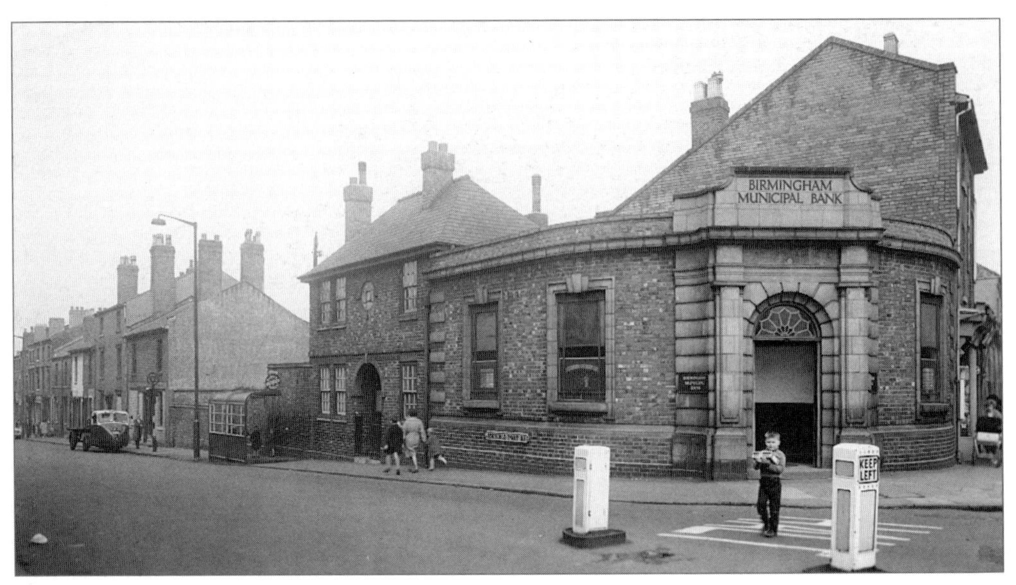

The corner of Icknield Port Road and Monument Road. The stonework above the arch on the corner building clearly spells out Birmingham Municipal Bank. The bank was one of a number throughout the city that were established by Neville Chamberlain in 1916 as the first municipal savings banks in the country. 'The real problem is how to make a man save who hasn't saved before,' said Chamberlain. The Working Man's Bank initially fixed the maximum amount that could be invested at £200, and withdrawals on demand were limited to £1. The idea quickly caught on and records showed it to be a 'useful means of collecting small contributions for the war effort on a large scale'. This branch opened in 1919 in a former National Food Kitchen, and this building replaced it in 1924. The headquarters were in Broad Street. The Working Man's Bank, which became the TSB, is now part of Lloyds. The bank in the picture has been demolished: perhaps the builders had money to burn as this is now the site of the fire station!

Roughly the same location, only this time showing more of the Monument Road side, 29 October 1962. The turret on the swimming baths can be seen at the far right of the picture. The ladies may well be discussing the news that Alf Ramsey would be taking over as England manager, or there again they may have been more interested in humming The Tornados' tune 'Telstar', which had just reached number one in the Hit Parade. One of the shops is Hickman's the greengrocer, and another well-known shop is Bill Landon's the plumber.

Distances are deceptive here, for at first glance it appears to be a similar view to the previous picture. However, all the buildings on that picture had been demolished by the time this was taken in March 1968 and the baths stand alone on the far right next to the former Dispensary. The buildings pictured here are at the junction of Hyde Road with Icknield Port Road, now the grass area in front of the Oratory School. Dee's ladies' hairstylists, formerly Mitzi's, and the carpet store are about to have the rug pulled from beneath them, as they face up to demolition. The carpet shop is advertising a 'Demolition Sale', presumably at knock-down prices! The building at the end is the Nag's Head.

The Dispensary building, October 1965. Myra Curley recalls: 'We used to go there, pre-1947, for treatment because it was free. I lived at the end of Bath Passage which ran between The Dispensary and the baths. One of the neighbours was Mr Parks; he was a boilerman at the baths.' Other people recall scabies outbreaks which always caused a rush to the building for treatment. By the time this photograph was taken The Dispensary had become the Ladywood Community Centre. It operated there from about 1951 until it closed for demolition in October 1968.

Nos 133–43 Monument Road, 13 August 1959. On the extreme left is part of the Co-op cleaners, which is next to Barker's car showroom. Robinson's the confectioner and Pritchard's the optician are the immediate neighbours. The top of St John's Church tower can just be seen at the end of the rest of the shops. The Mini came out the week after this picture was taken, and many people recall buying their first Mini car from Barker's.

This is the same stretch of shops from the opposite direction, on the same day. Woodward's stores dominates the corner with Wood Street. Next door the lady in black is looking in the window of Bryan's radio and television shop. The blind next door is keeping the sun off the meat in the window of Hipkins's shop. Woodward's Stores carries a blind bearing the name of Pearks, a former owner.

Nos 133–6 Monument Road. There is no date on this picture but the Co-op sold grocery, confectionery and also had a butchery. A slogan on the wall reads 'Foodstuffs direct from the producer to you'.

os 339–55 Monument Road, April 1960. The Rubber shop bends round the corner into Icknield Square. The 'indow advertises clothing for people hooked on angling. Other shops here include Reeves's signwriters and Jaffa's rocery shop. Just behind the dustcart there is an entrance to a courtyard of houses called Linden Terrace. The iop with a canopy is Capsey's the greengrocer, and a branch of Walter Smith's is nearby. The white building is ie Duke of Wellington pub on the corner of Leach Street. Ledsam Street runs off to the right.

Nos 316–28 Monument Road, 20 February 1958. This was taken three days before I was born and I now work in the building that replaced these, Ladywood Arts & Leisure Centre, formerly Ladywood School. The former Dispensary, by then the Community Centre, is on the far left and on the far right is a branch of Lloyd's Bank on Beach Street corner. The Bulmer's Cider truck is delivering to the outdoor, run by Mr Hancock, which is next to Shipley's toy shop and Betty's ladies' clothes shop. Hidden behind the lorry is a branch of Hickman's, this one run by Alfred Joe Hickman.

Looking the opposite way, 25 October 1965. Doris's fruit and flower shop is all boarded up ready for demolition to make way for the school playground. That week customers had plenty to talk about. The final stages of the abolition of the death penalty were going through Parliament, the Moors murderers were being charged, the Beatles received their MBEs and earlier that month the GPO Tower opened! That summer's Beatles hit was 'Help!', something that Doris probably needed. Two doors away Harvey's hardware shop was still trading.

Freeth Street, February 1966. Behind Monument Road was a mass of terraced housing, now the site of Ladywood Arts & Leisure Centre – the site of which is on the right of the picture. On the left stand numerous factories built along the canal which runs behind them. Osler had his glass works here and the William Morris Brass Works continues to trade from here, but without needing to use the canal. The low factory behind the Morris Minor was the premises of D.T. Hall, which made spectacle cases. The tall building is the former jam factory of Canning and Wildblood. The 'Jamus' as it was called employed many seasonal workers to top the strawberries and other fruits. German prisoners of war were also employed in the early 1940s.

At the end of Freeth Street stood Icknield Square, which had two entrances on to Monument Road. Here it is looking unloved in August 1967 – although at that time 'All You Need Is Love' was number one in the Hit Parade! The lady on the corner is Mrs Bailey.

Beach Street, 1968. Beach Street ran from Freeth Street to Monument Road. By the time this photograph was taken the new maisonettes on the Central Ladywood Estate were being built, and one block can just be seen at the end of the road, on Rodney Close, which was cut off from this side of Ladywood by the new Ladywood Middleway.

The Freeth Arms in Freeth Street, 25 November 1967. The street was named after poet and balladeer John Freeth who wrote a song about the opening of the nearby canal in 1769. The price of coal was halved over night. Freeth sang: 'Then revel in gladness, let harmony flow, from the district of Bordesley to Paradise Row. For true feeling of joy in each breast is wrought. When coals under five pence per hundredweight are bought.' The song was probably not recited in the Freeth Arms very often!

Happy families in Beach Street, 1953. The Adams family lived and played there. On the left is Colin Marshall, with three members of the Adams family, Anne, Lynne and Tony. Irene Adams's father, Billy Parkes, had a hairdresser's shop at 5 Beach Street. 'He purchased it in 1914 for £17 and kept it until his death in 1960. I and my brothers were born above it. The shop used to be open long hours, until 9 p.m. on Saturdays or until the shop was empty of customers. I was known as the lady who could cut men's hair and shave them with an open razor!' said Irene.

Michael Carleton, aged four, at play outside his home in Beach Street, 1946.

In the garden at 15 Icknield Square just before the outbreak of war. At the front is Stephen Cox. Mrs Plevey, the next door neighbour, looks on.

Ladywood Road at the junction with St Vincent Street. Ladywood Road runs across the picture. At the far end is the Star Billiard Club. The butcher's shop has the name A.M. Smith above the door, but was once run by a Mr Hanley.

St Vincent Street, between Great Tindal Street and Sherborne Street. Barber's tea was sold at the corner café. In the 1960s redevelopment the street was truncated, and this is now the location of the Ladywood Neighbourhood Office.

The Bridge Inn, Monument Road. The bridge to the left carried the road over the canal. The cast-iron urinal was a commonplace feature which people didn't want to loo-se, but it was all cisterns go shortly after this photograph was taken and today only the wall remains. There was a cooked meat shop between the pub and the post office.

The corner of Monument Road and Ledsam Street. The delivery lorry is outside the Bridge Inn. The impressive corner building, owned by Pearce Brothers, took full advantage of its location by having large windows on both levels. They sold prams, toys, clocks and clothes and were popular because of the 'club card': you had the goods and paid £1 a week on a card until you'd paid off your debt. Pearce's moved to the new shopping parade on St Vincent Street and closed in 1999.

Ledsam Street, *c.* 1905. The cyclist, who looks as if he may be a priest on the way to the Oratory, is cycling across the cobbled junction with Great Tindal Street, heading towards Monument Road. The square building at the end of the row is Belliss and Morcom's. The newsagent on the right has huge signs advertising BDV tobacco, St Julien's tobacco and Player's cigarettes. The block was 'the scene of a crime that shattered the whole country' which led to 'the perpetrators being sentenced to penal servitude for life'.

One of the shops featured above, *c.* 1910. It wasn't called The Old Dynamite shop for nothing! In April 1883, when it was a wallpaper and paint shop, an Irish-American, Alfred Whitehead, was arrested for having explosives on the premises. He planned to bomb public buildings, including the House of Commons, to create a reign of terror that would raise the profile of the 'Irish Question'. There were enough explosives on the premises to kill hundreds of people. Armed police were called in to hold back the crowd that had gathered. A police sergeant took the unstable explosives to Saltley sewage farm where they were blown up. The papers said: 'the entire press of the country have awarded the Birmingham Police much credit for their work'. Local historian Chris Upton, writes in his *History of Birmingham* that Whitehead's claim that he was using nitro-glycerine for hanging wallpaper didn't stick!

A family who lived in St Mary Street, 1937.

Johnstone Street and St Mary Street junction, January 1959. The dog is looking up Johnstone Street towards Alston Street. St John's Church is situated at the far end of the street. Note the road sign warning motorists that they are nearing St John's School. That month motorists were mourning the death of reigning world motor racing champion, Mike Hawthorn, after a crash on the Guildford bypass.

The corner of Great Tindal Street and St Mary Street, c. 1929–30. This was a shop owned by Mrs Gee. The stone inscription between the Rinso and Hudson's soap advert reads 'Ladywood Quadrant'. This is near today's Rodney Close.

Happy shoppers in Edward Street. According to Albert Trapp, who lived there, 'These are members of the Davies family, Eric and his wife and daughter Edna.' The other person is the original mystery shopper. She seems happy, even though the newspaper headline reads 'The loaf is to be 10½*d* next week'.

'amily life in Sheepcote Street, 1920. George Palmer owns the picture of his grandmother Lizzie and her son Sam, who was twelve, and later to be George's ather. Note the budgie's cage.

Beryl Hicks, aged four, 1913.

'his lady was a bargee: she was obviously dressed for special occasion.

This brilliantly portrays everyday life. Lizzie Palmer worked at nearby Hudson Edmunds as a brass turner. Her husband Jack worked on the trams. The family moved out to Coxwell Road in 1939. Lizzie and Ethel are taking advantage of the sunshine, in a courtyard surrounded by 40 ft high walls, as they peel sprouts for Sunday dinner.

The entrance to the courtyard of seven houses where the Palmer family lived was next to the Albion pub just behind the lorry cab. The car is outside Foxall's Café which was popular with workers at Baxter's tube works on the opposite side of the road. Adjacent to the café is the Hudson Edmunds' works with its large stone entrance arch to enable wide horse-drawn carriages to enter. This is how it looked in 1986. The row of buildings gained listed status and still awaits redevelopment.

Tony Higgs, left, aged nine, with his brother Tim, aged seven, in a Nelson School photograph, 1959. Tony says: 'We moved to Sheepcote Lane in 1954 and stayed until the demolition men moved in in 1965. It was in many ways a typical Victorian street, but it was slightly unusual in that the houses only ran down one side. Along the other side there was a continuous blue-brick wall. The wall separated Sheepcote Lane from St Vincent Street, both of which led off King Edward's Road. St Vincent Street was at a higher level because of the railway, so a flight of steps was provided to link it with our lane. The street contained a number of back-to-back terraces grouped around courtyards. We slept in the attic room and had uninterrupted views over the wall straight into the coal yards on the opposite side of St Vincent Street. By glancing to the right it was possible to see into the very heart of the railway engine sheds. My house disappeared to make way for the new Nelson School, but it is still possible to walk along the lane in the shadow of the blue-brick wall. On it is the faint reminder of the painted goal posts where we used to play football!'

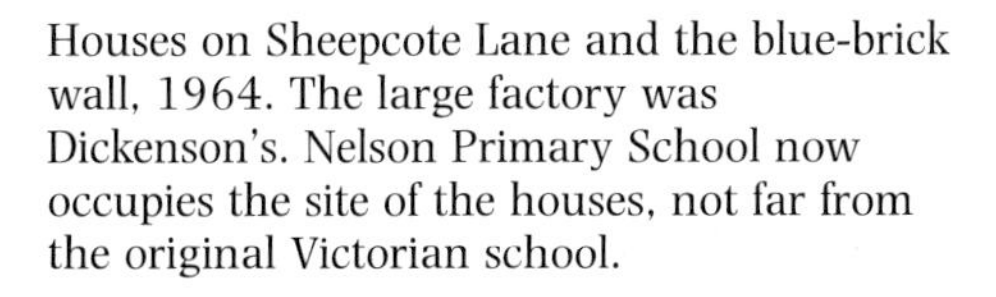

Houses on Sheepcote Lane and the blue-brick wall, 1964. The large factory was Dickenson's. Nelson Primary School now occupies the site of the houses, not far from the original Victorian school.

St Mark's Church in St Mark's Street was a sandstone building, and was consecrated in 1841. It had eroded to such a bad extent that it was closed in 1947. This is the wedding of Olive Smith and Raymond Wise in 1946. His sister Iris, now Mrs Carter, who loaned the picture recalls: 'We lived in Louisa Street and he was a foreman toolsetter. Olive, from Summerhill Street, worked at Veritas Electrical in nearby Edward Street. The church was a very old favourite of everyone in Ladywood.'

Maud Checkley married William Floyd of Bishopsgate Street at St Mark's Church in February 1939. Maud remembers: 'William was brought up by his gran, who is second left at the back, because his dad was killed at the Somme. My mother is on the far right at the front; she brought up eleven children. Two of the bridesmaids were my sisters, Edna and Violet. My uncle who was a superintendent at Avery's is the man in a dickie bow. Nearly 150 people were there and I was the first one of the family to have a do in the Infant School hall. Some people thought we were a bit 'oity toity because of it!'

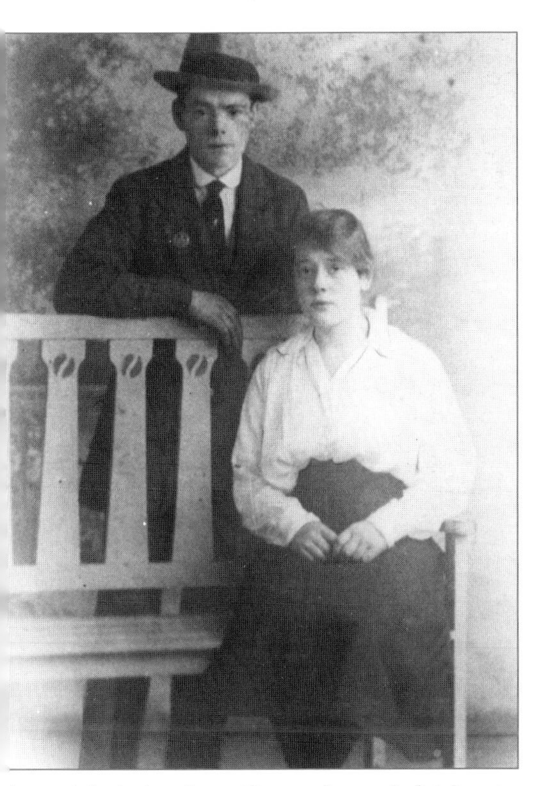

A special photo of my Nan and grandad taken in 1919. Nan was nineteen and he was twenty-three. The photograph has only been taken off the wall once since it was first hung, and that was to take a copy for this book!

Edie Faulkner on her twenty-first birthday, 1945.

No. 14 back of 111 St Mark's Street, late 1950s. Edie Faulkner, now Mrs Ockford, recalls: 'I'm in the middle with my two nieces, Margaret and Judith. I think I was on my day off from my job on the railways. I worked at New Street where I did several jobs including being a porter, an announcer and I also worked in the dispatch office. Their family worked at McKechnie's on Icknield Port Road.'

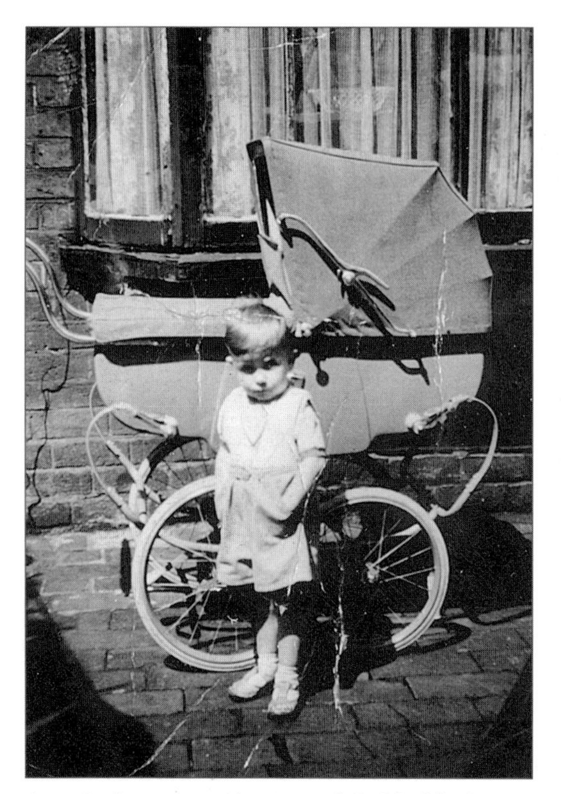

A typical scene at the rear of St Mark's Street, *c.* 1955. The child who lived there was Paul Wood. The houses here were three-bedroomed, including the attic.

Connie Jones, later Mrs Mason, relaxes at the rear of 100 St Mark's Street, 1949. She worked in the Jewellery Quarter as a jobbing clerk. Henry Mason recalls: 'The walls were later painted white so as to reflect some light into the yard.'

Children at play at the rear of St Mark's Street at 14 back of 111, early 1950s. Toy cars similar to these were made by Montil's in Morville Street.

A view probably taken in the early 1960s. The mass of terraced houses are on Anderton Street, in the lower left-hand corner, and on King Edward's Road which runs up the middle. The triangle junction is where 'little' and 'big' St Mark's Street join. In the centre of the island children used to gather to watch the lamplighter at work on the gas lamp. The Salvation Army used to play beneath it. The big building is the paint warehouse built on the site of St Mark's Church. The road which runs across the picture, about a third of the way up, is Monument Road. Look for the distinctive shape of the frontage of the Methodist church and the black arched roof of the Palais de Danse. The road which runs alongside the Palais is Ingleby Street. This links Monument Road with Spring Hill. At the end of it, on Spring Hill, there is St Peter's Church. Spring Hill disappears into the distance, crossing the railway and canal near Summerfield School. Near to it lies the sprawling hospital and, whisper it quietly, the former workhouse! Another school, Steward Street, is in the centre of the picture.

A similar view from the top of Durham Tower, 1999. Part of St Mark's Street still exists and King Edward's Road is now the truncated road on the right. The whole estate is called St Mark's estate. The burned-out factory is on the corner of Goodman Street.

St Mark's Street. The building on the extreme right is the paint warehouse which still stands today; it was built on the site of St Mark's Church and School. The first house next to it was once a sweet shop. Henry Mason recalls that the owner was 'a little old lady who complained a lot when we kicked our ball against the side wall, which was the boundary wall of the school playground. The author's mother Nora recalls: 'the shop was owned by Polly Johnson and she sold all sorts of sweets. We were caught stealing lollipops once and we never did it again!'

Shakespeare Road, from Monument Road looking towards the city. This road was probably built for the railway workers. The main line ran behind the houses on the right. St Mark's Street joins Shakespeare Road from the left, with a pawn shop on the corner. Further down on the left behind the corner is the junction with Anderton Street. Alexandra Street and Garbett Street join in the distance. Garbett Street got its name from a wealthy ironworks merchant, Samuel Garbett.

Anderton Street, 6 June 1967. This is Drayton Place, the first and shortest of the terraces near the King Edward's Road junction. Other nearby terraces were Exeter Place, Ferndale Place, Granville Place and Highfield Place. I wonder if LH still loves SN?

King Edward's Road at the junction with Alexandra Street. The little lad is outside Miss Haslam's greengrocer's shop. The other shop is George Harper's butcher's. The lad on the left is standing by The Bell. Another pub, The Vine, stands at the end of the row at the corner of Garbett Street, at the top of the picture.

Anderton Street, June 1967. If standing on street corners was an Olympic sport then Ladywood would have a few gold medal winners! The ladies had plenty to talk about, because breath tests for drivers had been introduced two days before this photograph was taken. Only a few local people had cars in those days and, if you had one, you wouldn't have used it to get to the pub because it would have been easier to walk: there was one on almost every corner!

Denis Daniels spotted his mother on this photograph. He says: 'Mom, Nellie, is the lady on the right. She was a polisher all her life and worked for Dickie Davies in Edward Street for forty years. When the house was demolished the family moved into Morville Street.'

The corner of King Edward's Road and Monument Road, 5 January 1956. Reg Clews was a cycle specialist, and he also ran a paper shop and toy shop opposite. In pre-war days he was an internationally known cyclist. The shop next door, on Monument Road, is Faulkner's sweet shop.

The corner of King Edward's Road and Monument Road from the zebra crossing seen on the photograph above, 20 April 1960. The boy is standing outside the cycle shop and the photographer is looking along Monument Road away from Spring Hill. Dickens's newsagent's occupied the corner spot; adjacent buildings included Ron Pharo the chemist and a chippie, a radio shop and a draper. The turreted building is Summerhill Methodist church.

The Co-op at Spring Hill, 1967. The road off to the right is Ellen Street. Part of the canopy of the neighbouring Home & Colonial can be seen on the left.

The Home & Colonial Stores at Spring Hill, 1956. This is a rare interior picture. June Spencer from Beach Street (who became Mrs Daniels) is pictured with two other assistants. Mr Cutheon was manager at the time.

Spring Hill, looking towards the library, 17 September 1951. Freeman Hardy Willis's shoe shop is next to A.E.R. Johnson's platers. The buildings behind Spring Hill Motors include a branch of Marsh and Baxter's the butcher, Jeff's the greengrocer and Wilkes's the chemist. In the far distance behind the library is the Palace cinema.

Spring Hill, looking the other way, on the same day. Johnson's have a large advert painted on their wall. The shop with the canopy is Gordon Mason's greengrocer's; Miss Zissman sold hats next door. Near the junction with Ellen Street is Allibone and Batchelor's hardware store and Selvester the chemist. The Co-op is on the other side of Ellen Street. Although there isn't one in this picture, a distinctive vehicle and associated noise was heard on the streets of Ladywood for the first time this month: ice cream vans with chimes had arrived!

Spring Hill. H. Barrett's was a confectioner and the Maple Leaf was a florist. The most well-known shop belonged to Watty Green junior, the bookmaker. All bookies were well known in the area. Elsie Humphries, now Mrs Rafferty, recalls him: 'He was a good natured man and very generous especially to children. We held terrific Bonfire Night parties in our yard and it was done through Watty Green and other bookmakers. He bought chestnuts, roast potatoes and some fireworks.' The large wall advert is for Finegan's Nip-a-Kofs, which were, as the name suggests, cough sweets. The tower of St Peter's Church can be seen behind the shops. The church celebrated its centenary on the day of a total eclipse in 1927. The original church was founded in the city centre before moving to George Street West in 1902, 'where there was a crowded population waiting to be shepherded'.

Spring Hill, looking towards the Hudson Cycle building and The Mint from the library, 14 August 1967. The library opened in January 1893 as a reading room and the first books were not issued until April of that year. In 1973 plans were drawn up to demolish the building to make way for the improved road junction. Luckily the planners were brought to book and the building survived. A plan was then drawn up to jack the building up on stilts and move it a few yards backwards. Following opposition it was dropped – the plan I mean, not the library!

CHAPTER TWO

WORK

Parker & Winder, Broad Street, 1873. In 1836 William Parker set up an ironmonger's business and later joined forces with Henry Parker and John P. Achurch to create Parker, Winder, Achurch. They didn't manufacture the ironmongery, but they purchased it from local factories and sold it from their impressive showroom. The tin baths on show in the upper window would have been popular buys for Ladywood people lacking indoor facilities. Broad Street was the company's home for 136 years.

Sheepcote Street stables, 1999. The building was erected in 1840, or 1864, depending on your source of information, for the London & North Western Railway. It was used as a mineral and coal wharf and as stables for horses which transported goods that had arrived by barge and by railway. Today it is a listed building and includes a variety of craft workshops and a pub called the Fiddle and 'bone. The pub is thought to be housed in an old school. There are also six of the remaining stables and these are being preserved as a tourist attraction. Wooden cobbles are used in parts of the building instead of stone ones. This was because they were quieter than stone ones and they soaked up the urine left by the horses!

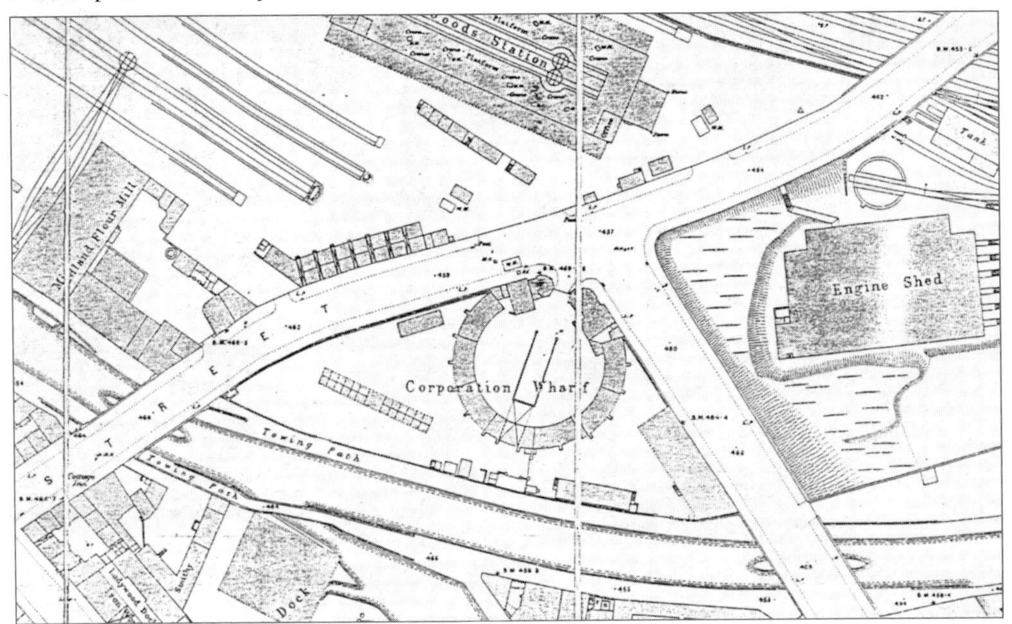

How the stables looked on an 1888 map. The horseshoe-shaped stables were listed as the Corporation Wharf at the junction of Sheepcote Street and St Vincent Street. The Midland Flour Mill and railway goods yard have been replaced by a housing development. The engine sheds on the left have been removed. The main railway line which links Wolverhampton with Birmingham still exists and the National Indoor Arena was built above it in 1991.

The arrival of the first barge in 1769 led to a growth in the canal network. This area of land once belonged to printer John Baskerville and he laid out an area of 'shady walks, adorned with shrubberies, fish ponds and a grotto'. Baskerville died in 1775 and the Ryland family bought the land. Early in the 1820s the land was laid out for a canal wharf and Baskerville's former house became a factory. The canal here was eventually filled in and excavated during work to complete the area around the Hall of Memory. The hall was opened in July 1925 and this photograph is dated 1936.

Lee Longland's factory on the canalside, near where Alpha Tower now stands off Broad Street. The canal system once extended from Gas Street towards the city centre and terminated at Paradise! The Birmingham Canal Navigation Company's offices were built on land now occupied by Alpha Tower; these were demolished in 1928. On Broad Street there were numerous industrial concerns which backed on to the canal at what became known as Old Wharf. Lee Longland, the well-known furniture store, started their business there in 1892. Wood for furniture was delivered by barge and furniture made in the workshops at the rear. Lee Longland moved to their present building, nearer to Five Ways, in the late 1920s.

The railways eventually put paid to the dominance of the canals, but eventually they too declined and the railway station at Monument Lane closed in 1934. Occasionally, however, special trains were run. Locomotive no. 46757 leaves Monument Lane on 3 June 1950. This was the week after ten years of petrol rationing ended in Britain and the cost of fuel for motorists rose to around 3*s* a gallon, its highest price since 1920. This train was the very last special to run on the line.

Joseph Walker Sands,

Coal, Coke and Lime Merchant.

DEPOT—RAILWAY STATION, MONUMENT LANE.

Entrance—St. Vincent Street, Ladywood.

LIST OF PRICES.—COAL.

Best Deep Coal ...	19s. 6d.	Cobbles and Rakings	16s, 6d.
,, ,, Lumps	18s. 6d.	Raked Slack	15s. 6d.
Shallow Coal ...	18s. 6d.	Rough Slack .. 14s. 6d. 13s. 6d. and	12s. 6d.
,, One Way	17s. 6d.	Fine Slack	7s.

The above prices are subject to alteration at any time without notice.

(Coal or Slack supplied in Boats or Trucks anywhere, at the lowest possible prices.)

COKES.

Durhams, Gas, Staveley Braes, Patent Coke

DUDLEY LIME, BUXTON LIME, SHROPSHIRE LIME

For prices of Coke and Lime apply at the Office as above).

The prices of Coal includes delivery within two miles of the Wharf.

N.B—Special Arrangements for Large Quantities

Everyone should lay in a stock for Winter

A coal advertisement dating from 1873.

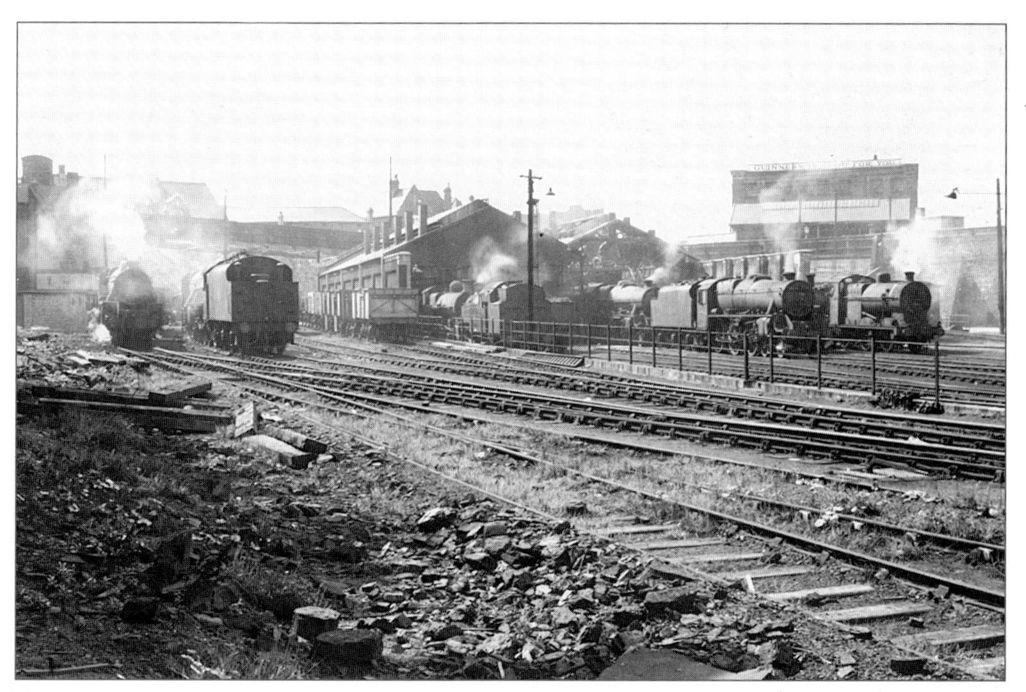

The engine sheds, *c.* 1951. Sheepcote Street is in the distance. The building behind the smoke on the left is now the Fiddle and 'bone pub, originally part of the stables complex. The former flour mill on the right bears a large 'Guinness is good for you' advert.

This is taken from the same spot as the photograph above but looking in the opposite direction towards the city centre. Today this area is covered by the National Indoor Arena.

D.T. Powell's timber wharf and saw mills, just after the premises was opened near to Monument Lane railway station in 1929. The sign indicates that much of the timber had been imported.

The railway cutting on the edge of Summerfield Park near Northbrook Street, March 1967. The line which ran from New Street via Monument Lane to Harborne was used for goods traffic until November 1963. Part of the route was later turned into a footpath, and this was officially opened in November 1981.

Oozells Street canal wharf, 1986. The street was 'staked and measured' and laid out from the canalside to Broad Street in 1794. The wharf was to become one of the busiest in Birmingham. By 1860 there were no fewer than sixteen coal merchants based there and numerous metal-working factories had grown up in adjacent streets. Over the years other interesting concerns included the Midland Spoon Company, the Midland Aerated Bread Company, the Birmingham Shirt and Collar Company and manufacturers of horse collars, cardboard boxes, boat nails – and a squeegee manufacturer! In 1860 Mrs Hannah Hobbis was listed as a 'bleeder of leeches'!

By far the largest factory near to Oozells Street wharf was the Atlas Works which, as the advert indicates, made metal bedsteads and mattresses.

The Atlas Works was founded by Alfred Wale, known as T.E. Wale, and William Daggett Powell. William began with a spiral spring company and he is pictured here in about 1905. The baby in his arms is his son Jack, who is now aged ninety-seven! He began working for his father at the age of fifteen and saw the company develop into one of the biggest and best woven wire mattress manufacturers in the country. Jack said: 'Business boomed with the development of metal bedsteads which were popular in hospitals across the world, particularly where they replaced wooden ones in hotter climates where termites were a problem! The company diversified into wooden household furniture and built extensive timber wharves on Oozells Street. Other metal goods were made, including metal handles which were used on the deck of the *Titanic*. One of the owners once went whale hunting and came back with a baby one which was stuffed and hung in the canteen. It became the logo of the company.'

The Atlas Works closed in 1958 and the building became part of Lucas's and the car tax centre before falling into decay. This is all that remained of the Atlas Works in May 1986. The bulldozers were soon to move in as the regeneration of the Broad Street area got under way. It eventually became the location of the National Sealife Centre. Wales's whales were repaced by similar sea creatures, including sharks which have a perfect view of humans as they pass through the country's first walk-through tunnel with a 360 degree view of the 'sea'. The canal island is not, as many people assume, a traffic island, but it is a device erected in 1941 to help the war effort. If the canal was bombed, stops could be erected from the island to the towpath blocking off the flow of the water, and the other two arms of the canal could continue to function.

Sykes's Timber and Saw Mill, Sheepcote Street. John Sykes, the son of a Quaker cloth merchant, established a timber business trading from premises rented at 1*s* a yard in 1862. Imported timber was unloaded at the railway wharf and taken directly into the timber mills. He used pine from Canada and mahoganies from West Africa to make the hubs for wheels on horse-drawn carts. The saw mills were across Sheepcote Street between the canal and the engine sheds in the area where the National Indoor Arena car park now stands. Sykes sold the yard in 1966. Notice the young apprentice in the background trying to get a peep at the new-fangled gadget called a camera!

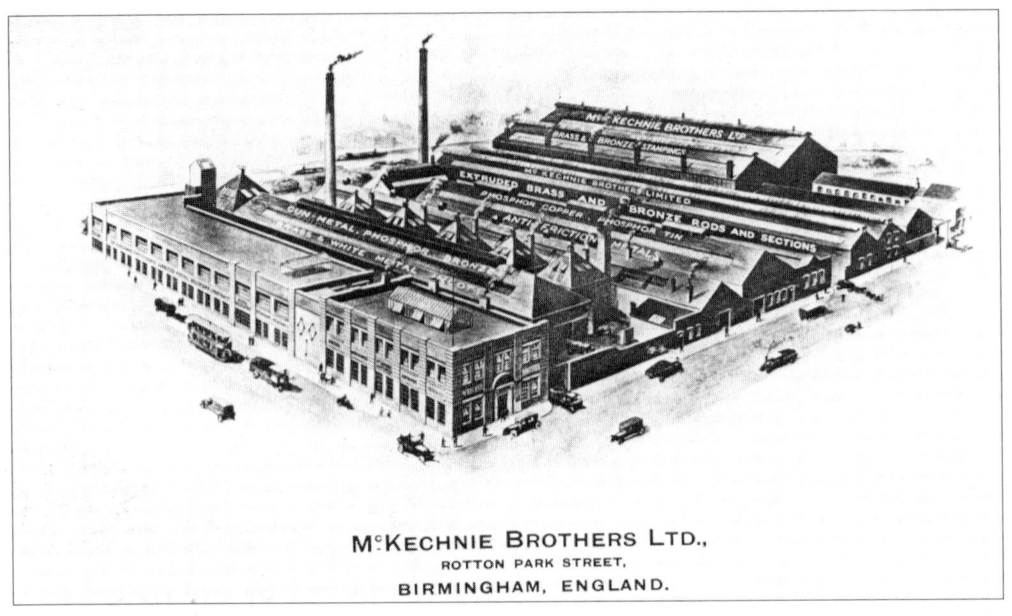

McKechnie Brothers' factory on the corner of Rotton Park Street and Icknield Port Road. The works was established in 1894 to manufacture brassware. At their peak they had branch offices in London, Manchester, Newcastle, Leeds and Bristol.

Stan Wood is one of the workers pictured here in the McKechnie's toolroom. The man at the back seems to be fed up and wants to get back to work, but the others seem happy enough to carry on with their fag break!

Docker Brothers began selling Stoving Black Varnish in 1881 in Bordesley before moving to Rotton Park Street in 1886. The label dates from 1910. Ludford Docker played cricket for Warwickshire and his brothers played for Derbyshire. They presented the Docker Shield for Birmingham Schools in 1886, and this is still played for today.

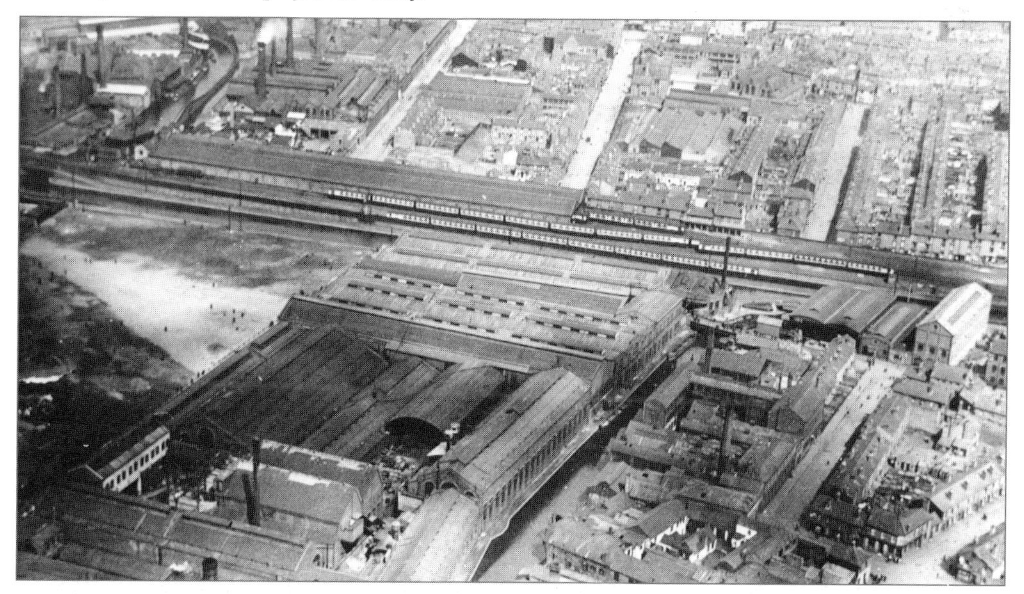

The site expanded at a rapid rate. The only open space here was known as The Valley and was used for cock fighting. In 1927 the factory was sold to Pinchin and Johnson. The incredible population density in the area is highlighted on this undated photograph. The mass of working men's housing to the bottom right is around Freeth Street and Icknield Square. To the top of the picture the housing extends from the railway to Spring Hill.

The paint firm was sold to Courtaulds in 1960, to International Paints in 1968 and then to PPG Pittsburgh Plate Glass in 1985. Today 13 million litres of automotive finishes are produced each year.

Nora Wilson, on the immediate left (who became Nora Bartlam, the author's mother) is pictured here in Wiggins's canteen with workmates. A Claus(e) in their contract was responsible for this break from work! Henry Wiggins produced nickel for silverplaters such as Elkingtons. The other waitresses are Clara Garrett, who is next to Santa, and seated across the table are Gracie Reilly, Flossie Hinds and Elsie of Marroway Street. The lady who is standing is Lily, who lived in Wiggin Street.

A tea break at D.T. Hall's in Freeth Street, mid-1970s. The company, the seventh oldest still trading in the city at the time, made optical and instrument cases. They have traced their history back to at least 1767 when William Hall was listed as making curry-combs, used to comb horses. The business has traded in Freeth Street since 1946 and expanded in 1966. Pictured are Marie Stepney, Pat Redfern, Daisy Warr, and Jean Redfern, who is Pat's sister in law. She once worked at Bulpitt's.

The manufacture of spectacle cases at D.T. Hall in Freeth Street. Hyacinth Taylor is the lady at the front. Behind her is June Rowe, and Mrs Sharma is on the far right. Other workers at the time included Janette Brookes, Paula Wilson, Bridgette McNamee, Winnie Parkes and Myra Curley. This part of the factory was reroofed and generally smarted up in the late 1960s.

Staff at the Mint, date unknown. The Mint moved to Icknield Street in 1860. Up until 1919 the pennies they produced had a capital H on them. This was in recognition of the Heaton family who set up the original brass foundry.

Staff at the Mint, *c.* 1900. The company dates back to 1794 and has the longest history of any mint in the world. The first coin produced was a centavo for Chile. In 1853 they started making copper pennies, halfpennies and farthings for Britain and they went on to make coins for over 100 countries. Up to 500 million coins are made every year.

Belliss & Morcom's iron foundry in Icknield Square, 1923. This was in the days when factories were labour intensive and machinery which was to eventually put a lot of men out of work was still to be designed. Here men appear to be placing sand around huge castings. The firm traces its origins to the establishment of an agricultural engineering business in Broad Street in 1852 run by Richard and Francis Bach. In 1855 they took on an apprentice, George Edward Belliss, and he later bought the company. Belliss developed steam engines and boilers and expanded into Ledsam Street in 1872. By 1884 he had taken on a partner, Alfred Morcom, who was chief engineer at the Royal Dockyards at Sheerness. This led to an expansion in marine machines. The works on Icknield Square were built in 1899. In 1906 Belliss & Morcom produced the first successful steam turbine and later developed diesel and gas ones. In 1932 it was reported that 60 per cent of the world's largest and most efficient gold mines used Belliss compressors.

A somewhat posed picture taken inside Belliss & Morcom's drawing office at the Ledsam Street premises, 1923. There is one female member of staff. There is a remarkable contrast between the two photographs. In 1968 the company became part of Amalgamated Power Engineering Limited and continued to make air and gas compressors. They made the compressors for Arianne, the European space rocket, to provide the initial boost to take it into orbit. Clearly this is a Ladywood company that has gone further than most!

This is a group of workers at Clarke & Jenkins's corset or stay manufactory next to the hospital on Broad Street. It was taken in about 1888, so no living person can remember any of the ladies, corset was a long time ago!

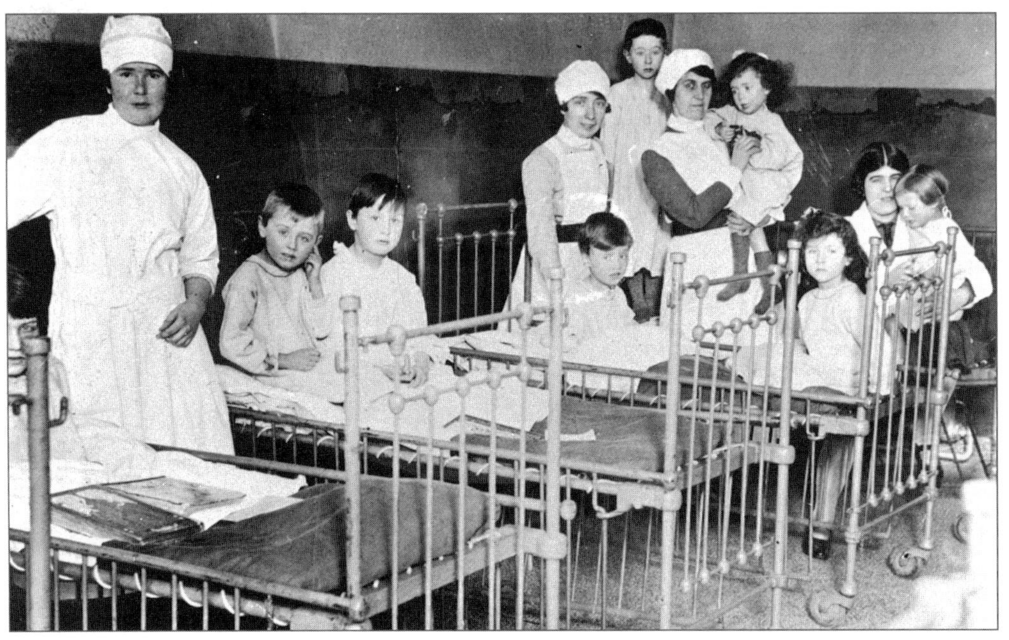

The Children's Hospital took in its first patients at Christmas 1917. It was called the King Edward VII Memorial Hospital and was officially opened by King George V and Queen Mary in 1919. The hospital moved to the General Hospital site in the city centre in 1999.

Ladywood at war. This publicity photograph was taken on Dudley Road, probably at the hospital, in September 1939. It conveys the message that we are ready for anything Hitler may throw at us!

Most definitely another publicity photograph, this time showing how to deal with injuries. Certainly the lady with a bad head is staying calm! How many of these people would have ever imagined they would do this for real?

May Mason was one of the first war-time post ladies. She is pictured outside her home at 80 St Mark's Street in 1942. Son Henry says: 'She worked out of Plough and Harrow Road and her round took her along Bell Barn Road. This was an area which seemed to be bombed every day.' Note the sandbags on the windowsills.

Fireman Sam Palmer who lived in Coxwell Road. In 1943 he moved to the new temporary fire station which opened at the corner of Broad Street and Oozells Street, in the Reeve and Stedeford building.

At Edgbaston Reservoir, August 1943. Members of the sea cadets attached to HMS *Vernon* arrive for training. A large barrage balloon was stationed on the shores of the reservoir and it became a well-known sight.

The sea cadets get down to some serious training, much to the interest of the youngsters on the towpath. The boat is passing under the Sheepcote Street bridge. The door opening built into the bridge was put in to enable the fire brigade to reach the canal quickly for additional water supplies at times of need.

Docker Brothers' factory was bombed in July 1942. A number of firemen were killed when a wall, buckled by the heat from the flames, fell on them as they were wading through paint which had spilled from ruptured tanks. This photograph shows the unveiling of a memorial plaque in 1948. The service was attended by members of the fire service and armed forces.

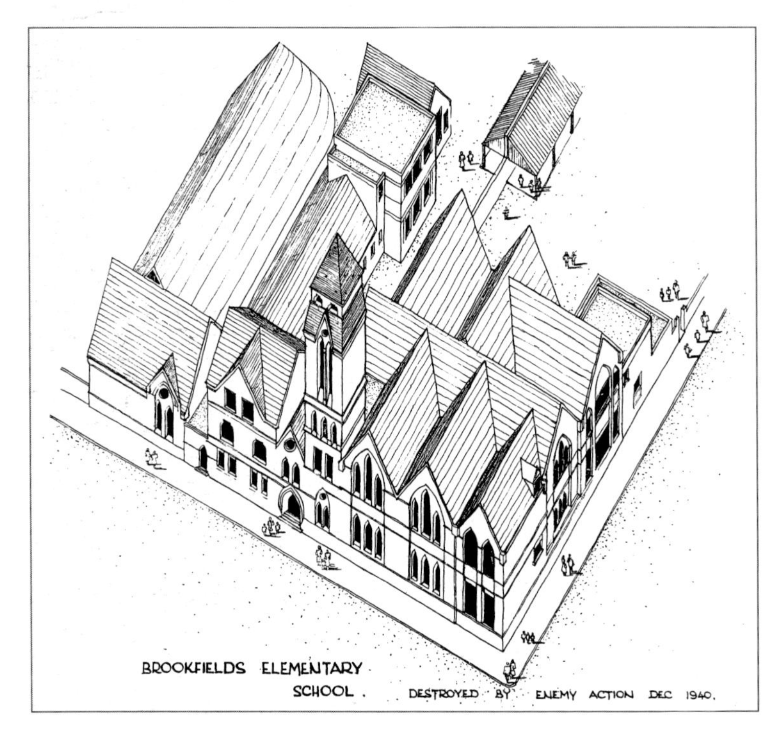

BROOKFIELDS ELEMENTARY SCHOOL. DESTROYED BY ENEMY ACTION DEC 1940.

Brookfields School, which opened in 1877, was bombed in December 1940. The raid that night was the longest of the war, lasting thirteen hours: 263 people were killed across the city. Work to rebuild the school began in 1948. The site of the original school was extended, to include the land occupied by houses that had also been destroyed in the air raid. It was occupied in September 1949 by 280 infants and juniors and was officially opened by the Minister of Education in October 1950.

Ladywood Police Station, 1911. This is the first known picture of the senior officers, who do not exactly look pleased to meet the photographer! It was taken in the rear yard at the station on Ladywood Road near to Five Ways.

Someone else who wasn't pleased to meet a photographer was Henry Self, who has the dubious honour of being the first criminal in Ladywood to be photographed for police records. He was involved in a scam to steal corn from barges by placing sawdust in sacks to replace the corn he had stolen.

The first police wagon was used to take criminals from the central police stations, including Ladywood, to the lock-up at Park Street in Digbeth. PC William Chapman is in charge.

Ladywood's first panda car, May 1912. It was a Wolseley, and was used by superintendents in the four central divisions. A police report said this vehicle was necessary because 'the area of the divisions is now too large to be transversed by foot or tram or even by horse vehicles'.

This was the scene on Warstone Lane on 1 October 1907 after a heavily laden tram overturned at the bottom of the hill, after apparently suffering brake failure. Two people were killed and seventeen injured. That week in an entirely different (but still transport-related) event, the German army announced it had bought Count Zeppelin's dirigible and the Count said he was going to build one big enough to carry 100 passengers.

Ernie Bennett with his clippie and an inspector. Ernie spent most of his working life at the Roseberry Road depot. Occasionally he helped out at other garages and is pictured here with everyone's favourite tram, the no. 70, which ran on the Lickey Hills route.

The last no. 33 Ladywood tram ran on 30 August 1947. It was replaced by bus service 95. The 2½ mile tram route opened in October 1906, and trams took a route from Navigation Street and John Bright Street along Holloway Head, Bath Row and Islington Row to Five Ways. From there the tram trundled down Ladywood Road to Monument Road at Furber's, then on to Icknield Port Road up to Dudley Road.

A no. 8 travels along Monument Road at the junction of Icknield Port Road. The shop next to the canopy is Hickman's. The curved building on the left is the savings bank. This bus is making its way up from Hockley. Children in particular enjoyed travelling on this route because it went under the bridge at Hockley, where all the interior lights would come on for a few seconds.

St George's School, Beaufort Road. The school was built on the site of Inglesant, the home of novelist Henry Shorthouse. Inglesant was the title of a historical romance which was very popular: even Prime Minister William Gladstone was pictured reading it. The school building dates from 1853 and the school catered for all ages of children. From 1932 scholars aged over eleven transferred to Osler Street.

This photograph of pupils at St George's was turned into a postcard. There is no date on it but a note says that a pupil on it, Harry Andrews, was later killed at the Somme.

St Mark's School, 1929. Edie Faulkner, now Mrs Ockford, is one of those at the back of the classroom. She says: 'Miss Tustin taught us for housekeeping classes. She rode to school on a push bike and wore khaki men's shorts that stretched down to her knees. She didn't like girls wearing tight knickers and she used to check and cut the elastic on them if they were tight!'

St Mark's School, 1935. Leslie Checkley, who is the second child on the right on the first row of seats, recalls: 'Miss Snow was our teacher and Mr Ridley was headmaster. We always started the day with assembly. A dividing screen was pushed back to create one big room for the assembly.' Don Newport adds: ' In the late 1930s the headmaster was Harry Walker; he was a keen swimmer and did radio commentaries for the BBC.'

A youth club group, St Peter's RC School, *c.* 1945. Father Donnelly is in the centre of the front row. The children include Nora Wilson, Edna Wilson, Audrey Alcock, Doris Alcock, Jean Thomas, Cecilia Jones and Mary Hollier, and also on the photograph are Mr Draper and his son.

King Edward VI Grammar School, Summerhill, 1911. This school at the rear of St Mark's Street opened in 1879 in a converted three-storey Georgian house as a middle school, and became a grammar school for girls in 1883. It closed in 1911 and the staff transferred to Handsworth.

The foundation stone for St Barnabas School on Ryland Street was laid by Louisa Ryland in 1860 and the school opened in 1862. Overcrowding was a major problem and this, combined with excessive heat and poor sanitary conditions, made for a stressful summer term in 1900. The school logbook records that 'the school room was crowded and the heat intense. Many of the younger children suffered badly.' Later it records: 'owing to a defect in the drains, so much solid matter had accumulated that the water from the flush cisterns could not find an outlet into the main sewer in the street.' The entry in the school logbook for 6 June 1901 reads: 'the caretaker has neglected to fill the school ink wells. As all the classes write on paper, work has been greatly hindered.'

The Oratory School dates from 1856. It was enlarged when it moved into the grammar school building in 1924. There is no truth in the rumour that Inspector Morse has just arrived in his Jaguar. This mid-1960s view shows the Oliver Road side of the building. The little building on the left is the woodwork block.

St John's School on the corner of Johnstone Street and St Mary Street, November 1960. It was opened in 1857. Anthony Spettigue recalls: 'My twin sister and I were born in 1940 at 1 back of 50 which is one of the houses right next to the school in the middle of the picture. Father was born on Monument Road which is the road in the distance. There was a Brooke Bond tea warehouse on Johnstone Street.'

St John's Infants School, 1933. Myra Curley, who loaned the picture, is the fourth child along from the teacher on the back row. The teacher may be Miss Price.

St John's School, 1930–1. The headmaster was Mr Dexter.

Osler Street Infants School, 1928. This was a special performance for Parents' Day.

Osler Street footballers, 1952. Back row, left to right: Mr Jones, R. Spooner, R. Richmond, -?-, -?-, R. Kelly, Mr Phipps. Middle row: C. Goodchild, M. Hopkins, -?-, -?-, B. Griffiths. Front row: J. Edmunds, L. Gardner, -?-.

Osler Street athletics team, 1945. Sidney Faulkner, who now lives in Australia, is on the back row.

A class from Osler Street School at the reservoir, 1942. Gordon Cull recalls: 'This was the top class at the junior school and our teacher was Mr 'Daddy' Davenport. The headmistress at the time was Miss Watson. I think there are fifty-four children on this photograph, but one class report shows there were even more kids in another class. There were sixty-one of them, and we could all do the 3 Rs!'

Follett Osler Street School closed in July 1972. Pictured are two teachers who together had taught for over seventy years at the school: Cecil Jones was art teacher for twenty-four years and Harry Rolin, on the immediate right, taught there for forty-seven years before retiring in 1962. The school was ninety-seven years old. The man on the left is headmaster John Welsh. The school diary from the day of opening, 15 November 1875, reads: 'each boy has to buy his own slate, copy book and exercise books and drawing materials'. Ladywood Secondary School, which replaced the Victorian school, was due to open on a new site off Freeth Street in September 1972, but a building strike meant the old building was reopened until the new one was completed. The Osler Street building eventually closed in February 1973 and remained derelict until reopened again in 1978 as an annexe to Ladywood School, because of a rapid increase in pupil numbers: this was as a result of the influx of Ugandan Asians, expelled by Idi Amin.

'he first staff photograph, Ladywood School, 1972–3. Back row, left to right: J. Jones, R. Newman, D. Lever, '. Pinkey, C. Doran, D. Lum, J. Hinsley. Third row: B. Dremza, J. Cottam, J. O'Hanlon, H. Lee, A. Bramwell, '. O'Callaghan, K. Warrilow. Second row: C. Jones, F. Norton, F. Shurmer, Mrs Lum, P. Watson, V. Broadhurst, '. Delves, J. Walters, W. Brenton, P. Mzimba, P. Cooksey, D. Watts, O. Davies, J. Doble. Front row: B. Punton, . Bailey, J. Redgrave, K. O'Leary, R. Perks, J. Welsh (headmaster), M. Heywood, F. Marsh, M. Gardner, D. Hambleton, . Barton. R. Mellor is not on the photograph.

adywood School staff, mid-1970s. Headmaster John Welsh is in the middle of the front row, flanked by his deputy eadteachers Marjorie Heywood and Hal Frankham. Hal was later to become the popular headmaster.

Ladywood School. Brendan Ormsby, who went on to play for Aston Villa and Leeds United is on the back row, second from the left. He made his league debut for Aston Villa against Derby County in April 1979. During the same season he was appointed captain of the England Youth team. Former teacher Paul Nagle recalls: 'Brendan's finest moment wasn't being selected for his country but being picked for the undefeated school staff football team!'

Ladywood School cricketers. Fred Cork is the teacher. Asif Din, the former Warwickshire cricketer, is on the front row, third from the left.

CHAPTER THREE

LEISURE

Trips out of Ladywood were rare. This trip was special for Nora Wilson of St Mark's Street as she celebrated her twenty-first birthday with her parents at Blackpool in 1952. Blackpool, Weston and Rhyl were always known as 'the Brummies' playground'.

Ladywood Swimming Baths opened on 27 February 1883. The *Birmingham Post* said they were 'an important anc desired addition to the sanitary and recreative sources of Birmingham'. They were more popular for washing thar for swimming. Once a week the tin bath by the fire was ignored as the trip was made to the imposing baths. Th water was obtained from a well and bore-hole 330 ft deep and was said to be 'clear and pure and somewhat abov the average of the town supply'. There were two large swimming baths which used between 3 and 4 million gallon per month. Myra Curley recalls the washing baths in the 1930s: 'You used to have to sit in a corridor then go int a little square room and sit again until your number was called. You were supposed to have half an hour but yo only had about ten minutes because of the queues. Friday nights were always the busiest. You were rationed to th amount of water you could use. They used to shout and bang on the door to get you to hurry up! As soon as yo were finished a woman came in with a pink gritty substance to clean up before the next person came in.'

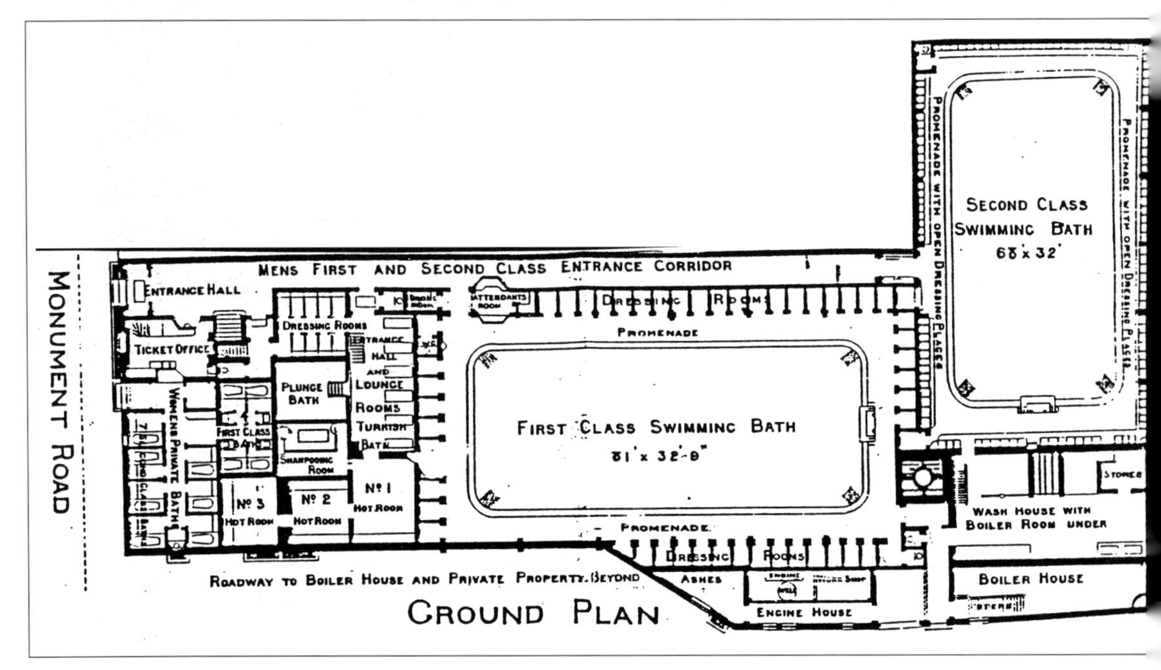

Just before the Second World War broke out it was decided to demolish the Victorian baths and replace them on the same site. The size was restricted by plans to widen Monument Road. This meant that a planned Turkish bath and a second pool couldn't be built. The new baths officially opened on 27 June 1940. The photograph above was taken on 13 August 1957, while the aerial view dates from 1987. The large building at the top is the former Crown cinema, now Bill Landon's bathroom centre.

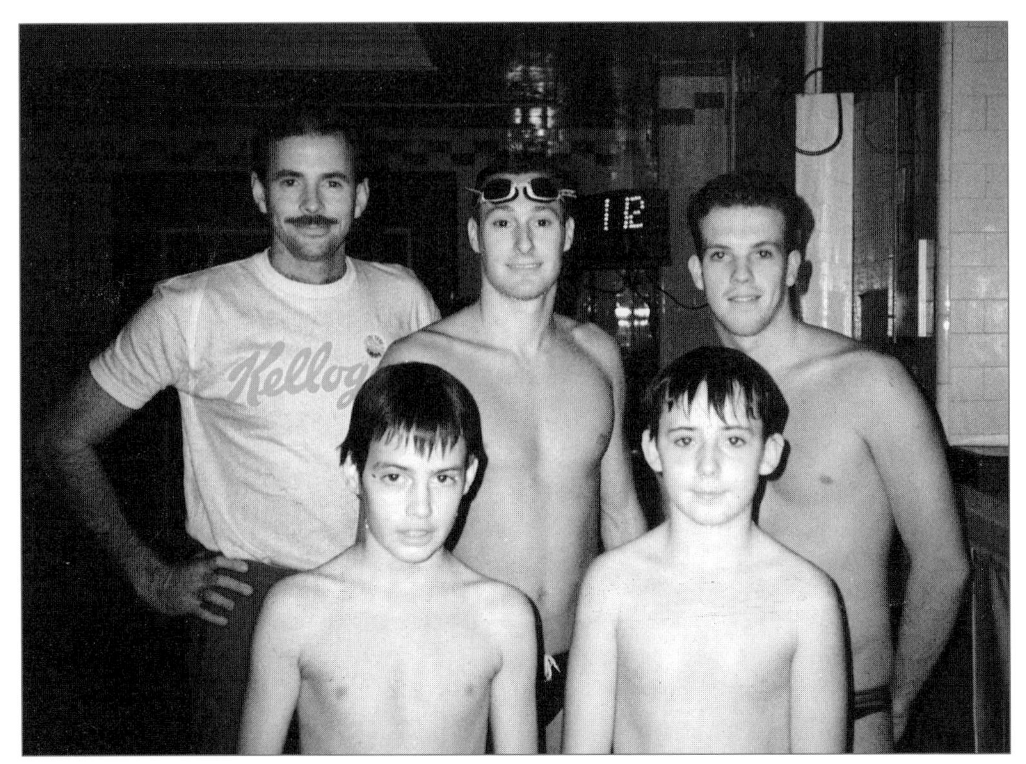

The baths became the home of the Birmingham members of the Olympic swimming team. Nick Gillingham, a former World, European and Commonwealth swimming champion, who was awarded the MBE, was the star swimmer at the baths. He is pictured here flanked by David Wilkie and Tim Jones at a healthy eating publicity launch with Ladywood School pupils Mark Bartlett and Brendan Brogan.

The baths were demolished in 1994 owing to structural defects and have not been replaced.

The Crown Cinema, Icknield Port Road. This opened on Boxing Day 1927. It closed in January 1961 with a showing of *The Angry Red Planet* and *The Amethyst*, starring Richard Todd.

Local bathroom merchant Bill Landon took over the premises eight years after it closed. This photograph was taken in April 1973.

The Regent on Ledsam Street was also known as The Ledsam. It opened in 1910 and closed in about 1959, when this photograph was taken. Today the Methodist church stands on the site.

An aerial view showing The Edgbaston on Monument Road near the Ivy Bush junction. It opened on Christmas Eve 1928 with a Douglas Fairbanks film called *The Gaucho*. It was a large building with seating for 1,600 people. The last film to be shown was *Camelot* with Vanessa Redgrave and Richard Harris. It closed in November 1968 and became a bingo hall for a short time, before being demolished and replaced by the new Church of the Redeemer.

The Palace cinema (the light-coloured building next to the hoardings) at Spring Hill. It opened as a theatre in 1905 and became a cinema in December 1911. Having suffered bomb damage in 1941, it later became part of Bulpitt's factory, and was eventually demolished to make way for the Rabone's building.

The Lyric picture house (just showing at the end of the terrace) was in Edward Street and opened in a former church building. It closed when many of the surrounding homes were demolished at the end of the 1950s.

Canon Norman Power, the vicar of St John's Church from 1952 until his retirement in 1988, owing to ill health.

The choir of St John's Church, 1962. Members include John Lander (vicar's warden), Molly Wells, Hilda Hall, Doris Finlay, Nan Cox and Rose Lander.

George Palmer's wedding at St John's Church, 1956. George says: 'This was one of the first wedding photographs that was allowed to be taken inside the church, probably because my dad was the churchwarden!' George's wife Doris Leaver lived in Icknield Port Road, and George lived in Coxwell Road.

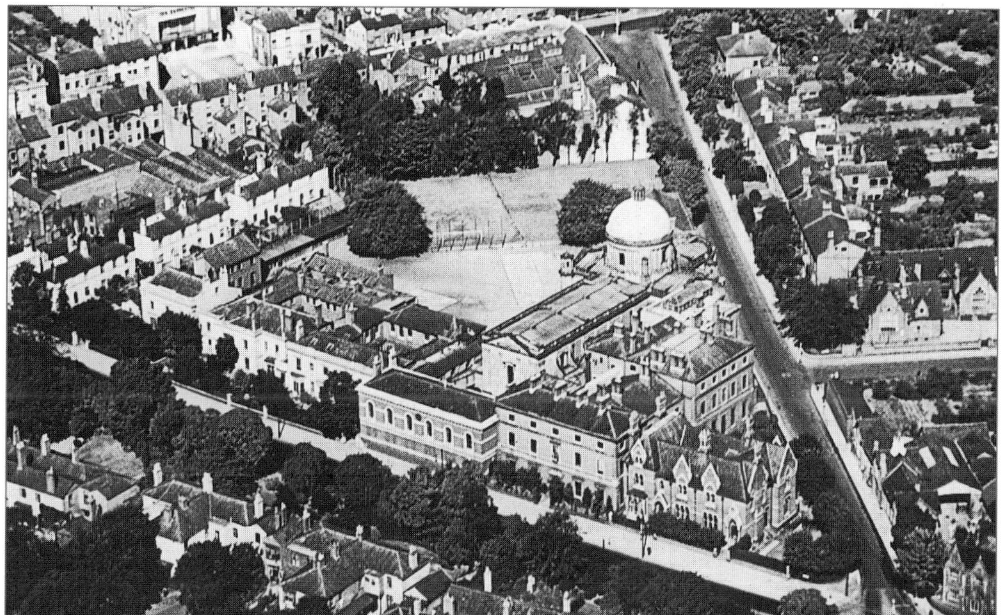

An aerial view of the Oratory, 1934. Hagley Road runs across to the left and Plough and Harrow Road along the right. St George's School is at the junction with Beaufort Road. The Edgbaston Cinema is visible in the top left corner. The Oratory was founded by Cardinal Newman and the present church was built as a memorial to him, and consecrated in 1920.

Lindy Carleton, aged seven, with cousins Rosaline and Jean prepare for their first Holy Communion in 1954.

On the way home from her first Holy Communion in 1965, Rose Rice stands on Monument Road near Beach Street.

The Church of the Redeemer,

HAGLEY ROAD,
EDGBASTON.

You are cordially invited to the Services on Sunday evenings, at 6.30, when the following subjects of interest to young men and women will be dealt with:

Nov. 13.—"Reading."
„ 20.—"Amusements"
„ 27.—"Companions."
Dec. 4.—"Business."
„ 11.—"Home Life."
„ 18.—"Sunday."
„ 25.—Christmas Service.

The Church of the Redeemer on the corner of Wyndham Road and Hagley Road, from a postcard dated 1904. This Baptist church was built in 1882 in thirteenth century style.

The 4th Birmingham Boys' Brigade Company Cup and League Winners, 1947. Ken Strangward remembers: 'We were the cup and league winners for three years running. We developed from the age of twelve and were sixteen when this photograph was taken. I later had trials with Chelsea and as an amateur I had a few games in their reserves. A knee injury ended my career. They gave me £5 expenses. That was a lot of money in those days as the train to London cost 16*s* 6*d*!'

The 20th Boys' Brigade at the Mission Hall in or near Icknield Square, *c.* 1920. Ken Strangward's father Sidney, a warrant officer, is on the extreme right of the front row.

The Boys' Brigade on a trip to Burnham-on-Sea, 1947. Back row, left to right: a helper, Joe Hoskins, Ken Strangward, -?-, Gordon Cull, Ron Bryan, Fred Gauder, Roy Tomkins, Ken Powell, ? Parkinson, Ralph Hickman, Ken Sheen, Frank Spencer. Front row: Ken Wheeler, -?-, Len Bryan, -?-, Clem Spencer, Evan Morris.

The 36th Boys' Brigade, Summerhill Methodist church: the Cup Final team at Villa Park, 1956.

The 36th Boys' Brigade, Summerhill Methodist Church, at a camp, mid-1950s.

The Palais de Dance was a prestigious and well-loved dance hall, although this view of it shortly before demolition doesn't do it justice! Situated on Monument Road at the junction with Ingleby Street, it opened in 1921 and was described as 'the sensation of the Midlands'. In about 1923 it held for the first time in the history of Birmingham a 'Wireless' dance. 'A band played at the Broadcasting Station, Witton, transmitted by wireless, and received at the Palais. Dancing therefore took place to the strains of music invisibly conveyed through the air. To have been present on this memorable occasion was an experience to be remembered'.

This sketch is from an advertising postcard, which announced the Palais to be the 'most luxurious Dancing Palace in Europe'. There were two sessions daily, from 3 to 6 p.m. (admission 2*s* 6*d*) and 7.30 to 11 p.m. (3*s* 6*d*; Saturday evenings 5*s*).

The Dance Band Championship at the Palais, 16 January 1934. Dancing continued into the war. Mr Bennett recalls: 'a bomb fell on a church in Camden Street and the whole building shook, it blew the dust off the ceiling, all the lights dimmed. The band kept on playing and we brushed ourselves down and kept on dancing.' Later in the war the building was used as a sugar store, and never reopened.

Sylvia Hunt of Icknield Street, now Mrs Duffy, loaned this photograph of her father Charles, who worked at the Palais in 1921. He is presenting a trophy to Lily Goodman of Canon Hill, who had completed a marathon twenty-four hour dance. Records show that Lily danced non-stop and covered 68½ miles while 482 tunes were played. Sylvia says: 'In those days we watched the dancers arriving in their ball gowns and tiaras. Even the large cars and taxis were a sight for sore eyes. If only we had a video camera in those days!'

Skating along are Bill Cokayne and his wife, who met at the ice rink. They became the Northern Midlands pairs champions in the late 1940s and skated regularly until about 1952.

A jolly trio, early 1930s. Ivy Maud Dabbs, on the left, ofte skated with her sister Pauline, who isn't on the photograpl Pauline is another one who met her husband there. Th lady in the middle is Beryl Hazelhurst, but the third i unknown.

The Ice Skating Rink at Summerhill was one of the most popular locations at which people from across the city spent their leisure time. *Skating World* magazine states tha the rink opened in September 1931.

Members of the Northern Ice Dance League, 1958. Ida Russell, who supplied the photograph, is in the middle of the front row. Her friend Mary Parry was one of many people to make the big time in skating and she became an international ice-skating judge. The famous Mohawks speed skaters were also based here, as was John Curry, the Olympic skater. This picture clearly shows the balcony from which the music came for the performance.

Ida Russell remembers the terrific success enjoyed by the skaters: 'John Curry is the boy on the left of the front row with dickie bow and jacket. He went on to become the first Briton to win the Olympic men's figure skating championship. Other people include Bernard Ford, the boy behind the cabinet; he won the world ice dance championship. Next to him is Janet Sawbridge who went on to teach Torvill and Dean, and Adrian Florence who is leaning on the cabinet at the front is now manager of Hull Ice Rink.'

Fun times at the rink, 1952. Pictured are Stan Homer with Trudy, Les and Stan's sister – plus an unnamed friend.

Bill Cokayne and his wife Iris, New Year's Eve, 1951. Bill says: 'This was a fancy dress party. Her father was in the jewellery trade so he got us a big bag of pearl buttons. We spent ages sewing them on and we won second prize. I think we got free passes to get in and we went for ages without having to pay.'

An official rink postcard called 'Youth on Ice'. Presumably you needed to get your skates on, so to speak, and get there early to secure a piece of ice, which is just visible in parts of this picture. It certainly shows just how popular the rink was! The card states there were three sessions daily – at 11 a.m., 2.30 p.m. and 7.30 p.m. There were also children's classes before the Saturday morning session, which ran for an hour and started at 9 a.m. The card added: 'Boots and skates may be hired'.

The rink closed in April 1964. On the final night there was a queue of over 800 people waiting to get in. Around that time the rink boasted two Olympic skaters and seven members of the Mohawks international skating team. Shortly after it closed the replacement rink, Silver Blades, opened on Pershore Street in the city centre. This building reopened as a roller skating rink, but this was never as popular as the ice skating and it closed in June 1971. For a while it was used as a car showroom, and this picture shows it as it looked in May 1992 – shortly before it was demolished to make way for a stationery store.

The Turf public house on the corner of Monument Road and Spring Hill as it looked on 12 February 1959. Customers inside were no doubt still talking about the death of Buddy Holly, who died in a plane crash the week before this was taken. On the left of this picture can be seen the derelict Palais de Danse building. The van in front of it bears the lettering 'Co-operative coke and other fuels, Coal Service'. The people at the bus stop are outside Leslie Smith's wireless shop. Near there stood Billy Pratt's greengrocer's shop. Don Newport recalls: 'in the war Mother queued for an hour for a rabbit to help with the meat ration. In those days if you saw a queue you joined it!'

This is the same view today. The tower block is Salisbury Tower, which was completed in 1968. The low-rise buildings around it were completed a year later and were named in 1994 after Ladywood cinemas: Lyric, Palace, Crown and Regent Houses.

The Turf was the venue for a popular entertainer who was renowned as 'the man who made King Edward laugh'. Bill Barrett, known in entertainment circles as Professor James Ware, lived in Camden Street. He was a conjurer and magician who visited racecourses and country houses, and entertained the King at Ascot.

The Steam Clock at the corner of Morville Street and Sherborne Street. This pub was originally the home of John Inshaw, a wealthy engineer. In 1859 he turned the building into a licensed premises and held an exhibition of 'a series of ingenious mechanical contrivances and working models and conducted numerous experiments on steam, gas and electricity. A steam clock was constructed upon an arrangement whereby steam condensed into drops of water which fell at regular intervals upon a metal plate, thus giving the necessary momentum to the works.' A large version was built into the wall. In later years the building was rebuilt and in 1910 it became a music hall.

The Glassblowers' Arms on the corner of Clark Street and Icknield Port Road, March 1968. Glass was made in Freeth Street, which is opposite the pub. The most famous glassworks was Osler's: they made the centrepiece of the 1851 Great Exhibition at Crystal Palace and candelabra for Mahomet's tomb at Medina.

The Mount Pleasant Club, 1947. These men are proudly showing their fishing trophies. Irene Adams, whose dad, Billy Parkes, is in the middle of the front row, says: 'Although they were near the reservoir they used to fish in rivers rather than the reservoir. They always went by coach as there were very few cars about in those days. Dad was very proud of the trophies and he took me out with him a few times.' The enthusiasm certainly rubbed off on her as she took up fishing and helped at the Ladies' World Angling Championships in Hungary, France and Bulgaria where she celebrated her seventieth birthday in 1994.

The Summerhill Tavern, 1950s. This was a popular venue with skaters because it was located near the rink. Stan Homer, on the left, is with a number of pals including Don Newport. Stan's father kept the Grotto pub on Camden Street.

On a corner of Cope Street almost opposite Monument Road station. Pub regulars prepare for an outing, but sadly no one knows where they were going.

The Nag's Head at the corner of Monument Road and Icknield Port Road, 2 November 1963. The buildings on the right are now the site of the fire station.

The Station Inn at the corner of Monument Road and Cope Street, April 1960. The railway station was opposite this pub, hence the name. The building on the right was home to the City of Birmingham Maternity and Child Welfare Centre.

The White Swan at the corner of King Edward's Road and Stour Street. It is not known why this photograph was taken. It certainly drew a large crowd to see what was probably a rare thing in Ladywood – a camera! Note the landlord's starched bright white apron and the little proud tough-guy boy on the right.

This is another unknown and undated gathering at the White Swan. The Swan Athletic football team was based here for over fifty years.

The ladies' darts team at the Stour Valley pub, 1954. The ladies were cup winners in the Birmingham and District Ladies League. Back row, left to right: Mrs Stanley, -?-, Barbara Steadman, Eadie Hewings, Mrs Hicks's daughter, Irene, -?-, Mrs Hicks, Mrs Cooke. Front row: Mrs Stanley's daughter-in-law, Irene Adams, Mary Cooper, -?-, Sally Hewings, -?-, -?-. Irene recalls: 'The league HQ was at The Gothic in Great Hampton Street. It was weekly league around the clubs and pubs. We travelled in all weathers even when the buses weren't running because of the thick fogs. We were very enthusiastic and travelled as far as Kingstanding. The final was held at the Holte next to Villa

The Stour Valley ladies' darts team celebration evening, 1949. Many of the people on this photograph also appear on the one above, even though this was taken five years earlier.

Enjoying a drink at the Stour Valley in the early 1950s are Mr Mac Sweeney, Jimmy Leaver and a friend. The Stour Valley pub was usually known as The Horsefalls after a horse which had a heart attack outside it in the late 1940s.

An outing, 1947. Irene Adams says: 'Most of the people were from Beach Street and the rest from Monument Road. We are outside the Horsefalls pub, but it wasn't a pub-organised trip. Hicks's sweet shop or my Dad used to organise them. Many of these yearly trips were to Ascot, but we're not wearing hats in the photo so perhaps this was to somewhere else like the Clent Hills. We used to have a great sing-song in the pub afterwards.' People here include Jimmy Hicks, Mr and Mrs Blower, George and Eadie Hewings, Mrs Stanley, Violet Hayward, Ernie and Eileen Parkes, Mr Field, Johnny O'Dwyer and family, Mr Wood, and Irene's mum and dad, Billy and Minnie Parkes.

It used to be said that there was a pub on every corner to cater for the men coming out of the factories at lunchtime and early evening and for the local population to use at night. This is the landlord of one of those pubs – Frank Deakin, from The Cuckoo in Freeth Street.

Seven drinkers who may either be in The Cuckoo or The Horsefalls. They are, left to right: Jack Lovatt, Mick Carleton, Ernie Fisher, Arthur Fisher, Lillian Carleton, Mary Fisher and Freddie Fisher.

The What Cheer! at the corner of Johnstone Street and Alston Street, 19 January 1959. This is now the area covered by part of Guild Close. The car on the right is in Alston Street outside Parkes's bookies, or to give it its official title, the 'turf commissioning agent'. This was the week that the BBC announced that the popularity of television was increasing dramatically and two-thirds of the population now had a set. Television had yet to make too much of an impact on the pastimes of the people of Ladywood. Regulars at the pub would be raising a glass to Henry Cooper, who had just won his first title beating Brian London to become British and Empire Heavyweight Champion.

An organised trip from the What Cheer! to Windsor, probably late 1950s.

The Warstone, near the library in Icknield Street, August 1967. The pub was named after a large boulder or stone which lies on the edge of the nearby cemetery and is believed to have been deposited by a glacier 10,000 years ago. 'Warstone' is a corruption of 'Hoarstone', which originally meant boundary stone. In the 1960s redevelopment the pub was demolished and replaced by The Florin which cashed in on its location near the Mint.

The Warstone Brew XI Festival League football team, 1962. Back row, left to right: R. Kelly, M. Sketchley, J. Farrell, A. Bradley, E. Johnston, T. Walton, A. Overton. Front row: M. Garvey, B. Parry, C. Jackson, V. Harry, -?-.

The Brew XI team with supporters, early 1970s. The goalkeeper in the middle is Tony Kelly, the father of Irish international footballer David Kelly. The tall player behind the lid of the trophy is Peter Harrington, who went on to play for Manchester United reserves.

The North Birmingham Six-a-Side Champions from Ladywood Social Club, 1975. Left to right: Bill Parry, Ronnie Kelly, Jim Cunningham, Ivor Davies, Mickey O'Brien, Tim O'Sullivan with the cup, Colin Green, Alan Shelton (almost hidden), Tommy Cunningham, and Gerard Quirke. The photo was taken at the venue for the final, Beckett's Farm, Wythall.

Ladywood Social Club football team, early 1980s. Back row, left to right: M. Duckhouse, C. Raj, S. Raj, P. Raj, -?-, C. Green, Chico, J. Raj, Leon, -?-, -?-. Front row: J. Cosgrove, J. Cunningham, Lloyd, -?-, J. Houghton, W. Quirke.

McKechnie's football team, 1951/52 season. This was one of many works football teams which existed throughout Ladywood. The player in the middle of the front row is Stan Wood. His father, Bill, was said to have been a founder member of the Rotton Park Gardeners' Club on Barford Road.

elliss and Morcom Cricket Club, 1919. This was the Departmental League '2 Top Shop' team.

The Prince of Wales on Cambridge Street. One of the window adverts is for 'Birmingham's best beer', which cost 1*d*. This used to be Birmingham's best pub as well: CAMRA made it their pub of the year. Inside it contained numerous posters of events which took place at the nearby Prince of Wales Theatre. A few years ago, however, planners 'revamped' the interior, and modernised it.

Ladies' Day at Ascot, 1950 – a trip organised by Billy Parkes. His daughter Irene says, 'It was the big occasion of the year and we all looked forward to it. There was always a rush for everyone to get their clothes ready because everyone wanted to look their best and enjoy themselves.'

The annual works outing to Ludlow for workers of Yarwood and Ingram of Ledsam Street. They were photographed near Church Stretton.

A works outing from Sykes's timber merchants in Sheepcote Street, 1925.

The first ever works outing from Docker Brothers' factory in Rotton Park Street, 1923. This was to an unknown venue. Note the lettering on the brick wall which spells out 'Stains, Paints, Colours and Varnishes'.

Sykes's staff off on a trip, *c.* 1900. William Sykes, with the white beard, is the brother of John Sykes who founded the business in 1862.

George Sykes's staff on an outing in 1921.

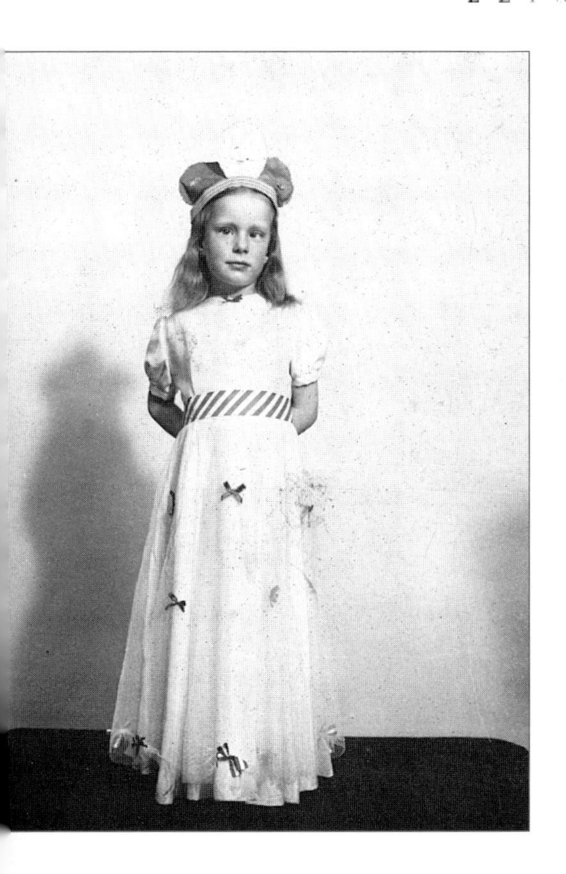

bove left: The Coronation party, 1953. Lindy arleton, now Dunnett, then aged six, recalls: 'it was great occasion and something we all looked rward to. The dress was made by my mother. It ad red, white and blue ribbons. There was a party t the school in Clark Street and I was presented with a box of chocolates.'

bove right: 'The Jubilee celebrations, 1933. Henry Iason, who is the tall lad with the hat, recalls: 'this vas outside St Mark's Church and the camera is ooking towards 'little' St Mark's Street. I remember for the free food; there were tables full of pop and akes. The other lad with the hat is Charlie Lovell; is dad played in the Salvation Army band. The two eople at the front are Rosie Bird and John Waldron. Iy sister Maisie is also on the picture. I look very raightuppish, probably because I knew I was aving my photograph taken!'

ight: VE Day celebrations in Coxwell Road. George almer recalls: 'A family named Poole organised it. Ve had races and prizes were given out to us. I emember Mr Poole: he made model aircraft and ven gave some of them out as the prizes. We had a reat big bonfire right in the middle of the road. here was a hole left there next day!'

The Coronation party for George VI, June 1937. It was taken outside 1 back of 12 in St Mary's Street. Kathleen Hicks who lived there is on the end of the back row on the left. Her father William is near the end of the back row. Other people include Beryl Hicks and Brian Miles.

The Coronation party in Anderton Street, 1937. Leslie Checkley recalls: 'This party was organised by Mr Ashmore who lived up the entry. He took this photo from the bedroom window of 2 back of 80. I was seven years old at the time and remember all the jelly and jam tarts.' His sister Maud adds: 'We had an old gramophone, a big wind-up one with a horn, and there was a big barrel of beer for the adults and we had races in the street. Each yard had its own tables, but for the earlier Coronation the tables were all laid out along the street. Spot the lad with his ears bandaged: he had mastoids!' The photo includes mainly members of the Checkley family, Maud, George, Leslie and Dennis, and the Willeys – Rose, Connie and Madge. Others include Albert Gurney, Peggy Ball, Edna Millward, Doreen Yates, Ivy Patrick, Maureen Patrick and Teddy Phillips. At the front are Olive Halsey, Alan Bailey and David Ashmore.

road Street, 7 July 1909. This was a special arch put up along the route of the royal procession by the Water epartment, outside what is now the Brasshouse pub. King Edward VII and Queen Alexandra passed under it en oute to open the University at Bournbrook.

l we know about this photograph is that it depicts celebrations in Rann Street to mark a royal event.

Police Orders
18th Decr 1859.

The Surgeon having advised that the Men on duty in the Streets this frosty weather should frequently rub their ears, (if impossible to wear any covering) until warm, to prevent them from being frostbitten.

By order of the
C. C. S
John Austin

An extract from the police records of December 1859. It is a note to the fourteen police officers 'on Ice Watch at the Edgbaston Pool'. They were employed presumably to prevent people skating on thin ice! A 1902 news-cutting refers to the skating club at the reservoir having 'a considerable quantity of apparatus for doctoring of inferior or cut up ice'.

A man without a cloth cap was a rarity at the turn of the century. These men were at the 'rezza'. The roller-skating rink, later to become the Tower Ballroom, is in the background. The reservoir was originally a pond known as Roach Pool and it was enlarged when the canals were built to help regulate the flow of water along the cut. At its maximum size it covered 78 acres and its 300 million gallons of water led to it being described in 1870 as 'the finest sheet of water in the Midland counties'.

dgbaston Reservoir, Christmas morning, 1909. The man on the left holds a sign bearing the initials BAYRSC, which stands for Birmingham All the Year Round Swimming Club. It also says Members Only, not that anyone lse would want to take part on such a day!

ne bandstand and Tower Ballroom, where many displays have been held. It is said that during the war years the servoir was partly drained to disguise its shape from the air, to fool enemy pilots.

An early Edwardian view. For many youngsters a trip to the 'rezza' on a sunny day in the summer was a holiday Sitting on the shore, sharing a bottle of pop or water and a few sandwiches helped to while away many a day. I 1918 a plan was drawn up to build a zoo here, and plans showed the location of the lions, ostriches and rhin cages. Luckily the plan remained on the drawing board!

The smoke pours out from distant chimney-stacks, but these are ignored by the stickleback-hunting youngster This postcard bears the following message: 'This is where we went on Tuesday evening, in the background th band was playing. You will have to go and see for yourself when you come over.'

Birmingham Rowing Club was founded in 1873 and members won a major trophy at Henley Royal Regatta in 1904. Another reservoir user, the Midland Sailing Club, was founded in June 1894. The clubhouse, built in 1909, cost £119 7*s* 6*d* to build. Many regattas and displays have been held at the reservoir.

In 1875 Captain Boyton of Texas demonstrated his 'life preserving dress'. The photo, although taken many years later, shows antiquated diving equipment. This book doesn't go into too much statistical depth, but we can say that the 'rezza' reaches a maximum depth of about 42 ft.

A different stretch of water is featured here. Canon Norman Power's daughter Angela recalls: 'This was taken at Gosport in Hampshire where my Dad used to take a group of disadvantaged Ladywood children for a holiday. He used to raise the money to take them through the church and about sixty children at a time went with him. Some of the children had never had a holiday before. He did this for about twenty-five years.'

This 20 ft high statue is of the celebrated tightrope walker Blondin. Blondin, famous for walking on a tightrope over Niagara Falls did a similar thing at Edgbaston Reservoir in 1873. A 1,500 ft rope was hung 70 ft above the water and Blondin walked, trotted and somersaulted across it, much to the delight of the thousands of onlookers. He completed the walk even though the rope sagged in the middle, and at one point his feet were below water! In 1995 the statue was placed on Ladywood Middleway at the junction with St Vincent Street. It points the way to the shops at a point where the Middleway is difficult to cross, symbolising the great divide that the Middleway became. The children in period costume are making a video to provide a dramatic reconstruction of the 1873 event.

ı March 1930 Carmo's circus set up what was described s 'the biggest and finest show Birmingham has ever een' at the Parade at Summerhill. The main attractions 'ere Togare the lion tamer, The Four Bentos, musical lowns, and Captain Anker on his high school horse. nfortunately the weather at the time was bad and one ight 1 ft of snow fell on the city. At 4 a.m. the tent began) creak under the weight and 100 men rushed to the ene. They couldn't clear the snow quickly enough and ıe canvas gave way under the weight of 100 tons of snow, ausing £20,000 of damage. The press reported that an lephant keeper had fallen beneath the feet of terrified nimals. The Lord Mayor attended the re-opening of the rcus, and Togare the lion tamer wrestled the big beast to ıe ground – that's the lion not the Lord Mayor! nfortunately Togare was soon to be seen wrestling with n even bigger problem because the circus was totally estroyed by an overnight fire. He was once again the ero. Togare helped to tend the terrified animals and oothed the burn wounds on the lions with raw eggs nd olive oil! Those that witnessed it described it as performance as thrilling as any of his public erformances'. Other animals were rescued and their cages 'ere towed away, some as far as St Peter's Church. Popular lklore has it that one lion escaped and was seen walking ast Spring Hill library. One of the zebras was badly burned and taken across the road with the elephants to the yard of the Nursing Society's institution on Summerhill, where they were nursed by the vets. Ernie Bennett who lived nearby says: 'it was an unforgettable scene; everyone was running around with buckets of water. The hot air was sending the burning canvas high into the air and sections floated down into our back yards. The tent was as high as a three-storey building. All the neighbours were out and they were stamping on the canvas trying to put the flames out. The flames from the tent were leaping above house height. I was really upset because I'd been to see the circus, I was only ten years old at the time and remember thinking Togare was the bravest man on earth. We were all petrified that the lions ould go for him!' Fire engines raced to the scene from Albion Street, Handsworth, Harborne and Selly Oak. hile speeding round Victoria Square one fireman fell off the engine: it didn't stop and the fireman got up and tched a lift to the fire! The best efforts of the firemen couldn't save the circus, though, and it never reopened.

DON'T FAIL TO VISIT THE GREAT MENAGERIE AND HORSE SHOW

OPEN ALL THE TIME FROM 10 A·M

TOGARE FEEDS HIS LIONS AT 12·30

Lady Eleanor Smith, writing in the "Sunday Dispatch," said:—
"I only wish that these fanatics could see the marvellous care with which the animals are tended, and the very touching affection they obviously feel for their keepers."

SHOW GROUNDS

THE PARADE, SUMMERHILL

OPENING WEDNESDAY, MARCH 12th, at 8 p.m,
and afterwards Twice Daily at 3 and 8
FOR A SHORT SEASON ONLY

PRICES: BOX OFFICE TELEPHONE: CENTRAL 1155

1/3, 1/10, 2/4, 3/6, 4/9, 5/9 REDUCED PRICES FOR CHILDREN ALL OVER THE HOUSE.

CHAIRS BOX SEATS

Chamberlain Gardens were opened by Neville Chamberlain (1869–1940), who was MP for Ladywood at the time. He was the son of Joseph Chamberlain and was born in Westbourne Road. He was our MP from 1918 until 1929, when he transferred to the Edgbaston ward. Chamberlain became Prime Minister in 1937 and it was he who announced that Britain was at war with Germany in 1939.

Chamberlain Gardens recreation area as it looked after the redevelopment.

Chamberlain Gardens, 1947. Beryl Hicks and Brenda Mitchell are seen on the edge of the bowling green, which was a secluded area with bushes around it. Ken Strangward recalls: 'at that time there were two tennis courts and a huge gravel area where kids played football every night. There was a brick-built clock tower which was about 20 ft high and 2 ft wide. We used it as a wicket when playing cricket.'

The rebuilt Chamberlain Gardens. The redeveloped areas with their blocks of flats had large areas of open space but often little play equipment. Dotted across the area were concrete play areas like this one. The flats were named after worthy citizens of Birmingham such as Kenrick, Dixon and Avery. Nearby, the three blocks which front Monument Road are named Clayton, Beale and Balfour – all of whom received the Freedom of the City for their political work.

NEW BANDSTAND, SUMMERFIELD PARK,
Opened by The Lord Mayor (Councillor H. J. Sayer, J.P.), July 27th, 1907.
ected by the Baths and Parks Committee of the City Council. Designed by J. Cox, M.I.M.E., Superintendent Enginee
Sta. Hall. Copyright by Geo. Sheppard, 12, Durban Road, Smethwick, Hon. Sec. Summerfield Park Musical Soc

The largest park on the edge of Ladywood celebrated its centenary in July 1976. It was land formerly owned by Lucas Chance, who had already laid out his garden in parkland fashion. The site of his home, Summerfield House, was chosen for the new bandstand which was opened by the Lord Mayor on 27 July 1907. The park was the first in the city to hold a bonfire carnival in 1960, which attracted a crowd of over 25,000 people.

NELSON STREET
Adult School Magazine.

VOL. VII. No. 3 | MARCH, 1906. | CIRCULATION 1,000.

WE HAVE THE PLEASURE TO ANNOUNCE THAT THE

NELSON ST. ADULT SUNDAY SCHOOL
Bulb Flower Show

WILL BE HELD AT THE

SOCIAL CLUB ROOMS, HELENA STREET,

On Saturday, March 24th, 1906,

ADMISSION THREEPENCE.

A LARGE NUMBER OF PRIZES WILL BE AWARDED BY EXPERIENCED JUDGES, AND A FIRST-CLASS

Concert and Entertainment

WILL BE HELD ON THE OCCASION.

A CORDIAL INVITATION IS GIVEN TO EVERYONE RESIDING IN THE DISTRICT.

Adult education was very popular in Ladywood. Clark Street Adult School and Nelson Street School were both noted venues. This poster dates from 1906.

CHAPTER FOUR

REBUILDING LADYWOOD

Awaiting the bulldozers.

In 1946 the city purchased 1,000 acres of land and drew up five Comprehensive Redevelopment Areas. The aim was to rebuild the houses, shops and schools, design new roads, provide open spaces and separate land uses. In the mid-1960s Richard Crossman MP came to Ladywood to see the conditions for himself. The exact location of this publicity photograph is not known.

Many people who lived through the 1960s in Ladywood get annoyed at the mention of Ladywood being a slum area as it creates the impression that the people had also entered a downward spiral of decline. Undoubtedly some did, but many remained as they always had – clean, honest, decent, friendly people who looked after themselves and their neighbours. The cleanliness stands out in this picture of a washing line full of brilliantly white clothes, while the surroundings are in a state of decay. Canon Norman Power argued that better houses, such as those near his church, were being demolished first and dwellings like these were left until last.

A view of Wood Street looking towards St John's Church, 1960. The road pattern was being drastically altered at the time. Rann Street didn't run across here any more, and the outline shape of the Ladywood Middleway can be seen curving round towards Monument Road.

This is a wider view than the one above. The photographer is standing with his back to St Vincent Street, looking along Wood Street towards Monument Road. St John's Church is the large building in the row on the left of the picture. The outlines of Rann Street and Alston Street can just about be picked out. Monument Road runs across the top of the picture. The swimming baths and the Community Centre are on the far right.

Great Tindal Street, 17 November 1960. Gilbert Harding and Clark Gable had both passed away that week. Soon these buildings would also be gone with the wind.

Redevelopment left Ladywood with holes not seen since the last bombs dropped in the war. Here children play alongside Monument Road near Beach Street, as the new road that was to become the Ladywood Middleway was built. One of the subways under it was dug at this spot.

Ladywood Road, 22 August 1961. The police station was about to be demolished, but the two buildings next to it, the almshouses and the hospital, were to escape the bulldozers. The almshouses were erected in 1859 for 'poor women, spinsters or a widow of good character who had lived in Birmingham for not less than five years'. At this time in Berlin a wall was being built, while in Ladywood a road was being cut which would have a similar, but unintentional, effect of dividing the area in two. The almshouses remain largely unaltered; by contrast the hospital has closed and the site is, at the time of writing, being turned into a huge entertainment complex. The listed frontage of the hospital building is being incorporated into the new centre.

The view over Five Ways, 22 August 1968. The police station had gone and Ladywood Road was in the process of being made into Ladywood Middleway. Along it the almshouses and hospital can be seen, and on the opposite side of the road the housing remaining around parts of Ruston Street. Further along the Middleway Gilby Road high-rise estate had been completed. The square of housing next to Auchinleck House at Five Ways was around Bishopsgate Street and Tennant Street. Five Ways roundabout was yet to be constructed.

The mass of terraced housing on the right made way for the Gilby Road estate, and Blythe Street, Rawlins Street and Friston Street disappeared. Later a new Rawlins Street was constructed and Friston Avenue was created nearer to Five Ways. A tower block off St Vincent Street became Blythe House. The main building in the picture is the Children's Hospital. Note the lower housing density in the area off Francis Road on the left.

The housing awaiting demolition is on Wood Street. St Vincent Street runs across the lower left-hand corner. The other roads are Rann Street, Alston Street and St Mary Street. Ladywood Middleway was to be cut across this area. Anthony Spettigue recalls: 'The building behind the large tree is the Gospel Hall on Rann Street, which was run by a Mr Lucas. We went there every Sunday. Mr West was one of the teachers.' The towers of St John's Church and Osler Street School can be seen in the distance. Norman Power said that the large areas of derelict land and half-demolished houses degraded the district.

Ladywood Middleway, *c.* 1968. The housing in the Wood Street areas awaits demolition. Much of the rest of the area is made up of high- and medium-rise blocks: most dominant are those in the centre of the picture on Gilby Road. The new St John's School is surrounded by acres of open space. The Chamberlain Gardens estate is in the bottom left-hand corner and the hospital is in the other lower corner. What is noticeable is the vast amount of open space. In Ladywood there were only 2 acres of open space before redevelopment, compared with nearly 50 acres afterwards!

St George's School on Beaufort Road has a new neighbour in the shape of one of the blocks on Chamberlain Gardens estate. Norman Power argued that such blocks were in danger of destroying a caring community, and lacked a mixture of social classes.

The Ladywood Middleway takes shape as part of the bridge over the canal is put in on 20 August 1968. This part of the road was completed in 1972.

St Vincent Street, 25 October 1964. St John's School was being planned for the space next to the white car. Sandie Shaw was singing 'Always Something There To Remind Me' at the time this was taken. Unfortunately there is nothing there to remind us of the view any more, as even the tower block, Blythe House, has been demolished, and it wasn't even completed until 1965!

Ladywood Middleway takes shape in the early 1960s. In the distance is the 1930s estate and behind it on the opposite side of Broad Street a crane towers above Auchinleck House, which was completed at Five Ways in 1964. The Five Ways roundabout opened in 1971, but the first section of the Middleway was opened earlier; from Five Ways to Morville Street in April 1967, extending to Ledsam Street, passing this location to Spring Hill, in 1972.

The Gilby Road estate from Ladywood Middleway, April 1992. By now the blocks had seriously deteriorated and plans were being drawn up to obtain funding for their demolition. The estate had 67 flats, 166 maisonettes and 48 one-bedroom flats.

This view, during construction, was taken from Ladywood Road at a spot which is now behind today's police station. The entrance cut into the pavement was for the Beaufort Garage. The last remaining houses on the left were on St Vincent Street. The tower block is Truro Tower.

Lincoln Tower, an eleven-storey block at the end of the Gilby Road estate, was completed in 1968. It was an attempt to increase the population density of the area, which was reduced dramatically as a result of the demolition of the densely packed terraced houses: 24,400 people lived in Ladywood before the planners moved in and today this figure has almost halved.

Gilby Road, 6 July 1959. Nightingale House is at the end. Other blocks were Colette House, Fry House and Cavell House – reflecting their nearness to the hospital.

The Gilby Road estate, *c.* 1972. More impressive is the vast expanse of Edgbaston Reservoir. What remains of Ladywood Road runs up the middle of the picture; it becomes Reservoir Road at the junction of Monument Road. The remains of Osler Street School can be seen on the expanse of derelict land in front of the 'rezza'. Between it and St John's Church is the old Oratory School. The new fire station can be seen across the Middleway from the church and the new Ladywood School lies next to it. The chimney of the swimming baths can just be seen between the two buildings, partly hidden by one of the tower blocks.

The last of the houses being demolished on Wood Street. This is the site of Holywell Close.

Wells Tower and Brecon Tower nearing completion in the heart of the new Ladywood, 1964. Each block has over ninety flats and is sixteen storeys high. Other tower blocks in Ladywood are called Truro, Lincoln, Salisbury, Durham and Canterbury: they were meant to be the new cathedrals of the sky and so were named after cathedral cities. The nearby maisonettes were completed in 1966.

This aerial view shows the blocks centred around Allensmoor House, Ploughfield House and Hereford House. Note the fully used washing areas for clothes. The road which cuts diagonally across the picture is St Vincent Street. In the lower left corner St John's School stands alone. The area opposite was to become the new shopping parade and Methodist church, which was built on the site of the Regent cinema on the corner of Ledsam Street. The railway, with the remains of the flour mill, is visible near the horseshoe-shaped stables, which are now part of The Roundhouse public house and craft centre. Above lies the densely packed housing around St Mark's Street, which was awaiting arrival of the bulldozers.

The newly opened six-storey Allensmoor House on Ladycroft seen from Browning Street, July 1959. Note the traditional Birmingham lamppost.

Pat Roach, the wrestler turned actor who used to live in Garbett Street and Shakespeare Road, is seen here outside Allensmoor House as he says, 'auf wiedersehen pet' to the block! He wrestled with a large crane and carried out the first ceremonial knocking out of the bricks to publicise a regeneration programme in April 1987. The mixture of houses and flats were demolished because of their unpopularity, owing to poor heating, poor ventilation and dampness. The block was replaced by the Neighbourhood Office.

Mrs G. Wilson with one of her daughters, Kathleen, and Pat Roach. Mrs Wilson was the oldest person to have moved out of Allensmoor House and into a nearby property. Her new house on the corner of Ledsam Street was a maisonette block that had been turned into houses in a process called 'top lopping'.

Hereford House on Ledsam Street was demolished in April 1990. It was replaced by Housing Association houses.

The 1990s hasn't just seen the demolition of tower blocks. This house was also demolished in 1994. It was the only remaining Victorian dwelling on Duchess Road. J.R.R. Tolkien once lived nearby, and some people campaigned for this delightful building to be turned into a Tolkien museum.

The fringes of Ladywood have also seen many changes in recent years, none more so than the area off Broad Street where the International Convention Centre and Brindleyplace have been built. The ICC site was once occupied by the Prince of Wales theatre and Bingley Hall. In the early years Bingley Hall built up a reputation for its cattle shows. This sketch shows the Birmingham and Midland Counties Agricultural Show which was held at Bingley Hall in December 1850. Edie Ockford recalls: 'Even in the years building up to the war the shows were popular. They used to give the cattle's milk away and as kids we used to take buckets, jugs and even teapots to the shows and get them filled up!'

This is part of the Birmingham Co-operative Society's Jubilee Exhibition, held at Bingley Hall in 1931. Here the grocery display takes centre stage. The signs include 'Shoe repairing by experts at Birmingham's lowest prices' and 'Having tried the rest, send to the best laundry'. Bingley Hall was always associated with the long-running Ideal Home exhibitions, which were packed with home gadget-hunting Brummies eager to improve their lives.

).T. Powell's saw mills and timber yards on King Alfred's Place, probably mid-1920s. King Alfred's Place is now he front door of the ICC. KAP, as it was usually known, was cut through land belonging to the King Edward's oundation and was named after the King of Wessex. The Queen opened the ICC in June 1991.

t Peter's Roman Catholic Church uring demolition, 18 February 971. The church had been closed or safety reasons in 1969. The site vas a car park for many years until vork started on the ICC. The hurch dated from 1786. The urial ground, the first Catholic emetery in Birmingham, was stablished in 1826. During onstruction of the ICC the remains f the bodies were dug up and re-nterred. Church records suggested hat 577 bodies should have been ecovered, but over 1,160 were ound and removed! It has been iggested that the mass grave was ecessary because of an bnormally high death rate, ossibly caused by a quick-preading disease, maybe cholera r a plague. The building on the ght is the former Brewmaster's ouse which was built in about 815; it has been restored to its riginal condition and stands eside the ICC.

Excavation work gets under way for the Symphony Hall, part of the ICC complex, in May 1987. (The Repertory Theatre is in the background.) The first sod of earth was removed in March 1987; 200,000 tonnes of sand and rock were removed and over 700 holes were bored for the foundations. About 7,000 tonnes of steel reinforcements and 55,000 cubic metres of concrete were used in the construction: apparently that's enough concrete to fill 518 double-decker buses.

Pupils from Ladywood School took part in a video project to chart the progress of the Broad Street Redevelopment Area. Here they are pictured in front of the Brewmaster's House in what was the graveyard of St Peter's Church. Pupils include Delroy Lee, Darren Cannan, Mark Bartlett and Mark Bagnall.

The site of the National Indoor Arena, May 1986. The train is entering the tunnel to New Street having travelled from Wolverhampton. The tunnel entrance was designed by George Stephenson and built between 1846 and 1847. The scrapyard was due to close. King Edward's Road is on the left.

Adam Iche and Brendan Higgins (with camera) present one of Ladywood School's video news programmes from the National Indoor Arena. This was part of the 'topping out' ceremony held on 12 July 1990. A sprig of yew was planted in the concrete at the highest point of the building to ward off evil spirits. The news team are standing on the concrete struts which would eventually support the arena floor. Their position is roughly just above the rear of the train shown on the picture above. The £51 million arena was opened by Linford Christie in October 1991.

Three hundred pupils from schools across Ladywood and Lee Bank sang for the Queen on 12 June 1991 when she officially opened the ICC. Pictured in celebratory mood are some of the pupils from Summerfield Junior School in front of the 'Forward' statue, which depicts the changing face of Birmingham.

Here comes Her Majesty, accompanied by the Lord Mayor Councillor Bill Turner, who is a resident of Ladywood.

On Friday 28 May 1988 Ladywood made national headlines when 140 firefighters fought one of the largest blazes seen in Birmingham since the war. The fire broke out at Taymer Plastics in Ledsam Street and spread into the adjoining premises of Alan Silverwood's aluminium manufacturers, and it also affected smaller businesses in the block – once the home of Belliss & Morcom. A huge pall of thick black toxic smoke from the burning plastics hung across the city. At the height of the blaze over a third of the entire West Midlands Fire Service's appliances were at the scene. Firefighters even arrived from Wolverhampton and Oldbury. A total of twenty jets and three hydraulic platforms were used. Two water pumps took water from the canal. The fire was only officially 'booked correct' eight days after the incident when *The Ladywood Bugle*, the newspaper of Ladywood School, did a special report on the incident. One worker at Silverwood's, George Taylor, told the reporters: 'We were doing a big order for Japan and had enough aluminium on site to make about 3,000 saucepans.' He added: 'I've been here for eighteen years and suddenly the place I knew so well has gone. It is beyond belief.'

THE LADYWOOD BUGLE

You'll find us where the action is.

140 FIREMEN IN LEDSAM STREET BLAZE DRAMA

NEWS FROM IN AND AROUND LADYWOOD SCHOOL

FREETH STREET BIRMINGHAM B16 0QT

10p

Ladywood School closed in July 1990. These are the remaining pupils with teachers and headmaster Jeremy Richmond.

The Kilby and Lighthorne Avenues housing estate built in 1967 now covers the site of the former railway goods yards – as seen on the map on p. 50. Only the canal remains. Today it sees more recreational than industrial use. The names reflect historical links with the Ryland family: Lighthorne is a Warwickshire village where the family owned land. Across Ladywood the streets off Icknield Port Road are all named after places in Warwickshire: Marroway Street, Coplow Street and Barford Road all reflect the link.

The corner of Grosvenor Road West and Ladywood Road, April 1960. The lady crossing Ladywood Road is heading towards the Powell and Heath registry office for servants and Percival Swann's shop is on the corner. The shadow in the road is being cast by the police station. 'No waiting this side today' is indicated by the circular road sign. The corner shop adverts are for a range of goods including Danish bacon, Zebrite and Player's cigarettes.

From the same viewpoint, May 1999. This is now the car park attached to Tesco. The Tesco site and associated office developments opened in 1976. It was planned to have fifty-nine shops, an entertainment zone with a 1,100 seat cinema, and a thirty-three-storey block of flats, but plans for this fell through in 1965. A multi-screen cinema complex is now being built on the opposite side of the road.

The shops on Icknield Port Road near to the junction with Monument Road, October 1962. The white-fronted one is Mrs Nevin's fish and chip shop. Presumably it had been doing less and less trade as the demolition teams chipped away at surrounding housing, and before long it too would have had its chips. Next door stood a household and fancy goods shop.

The fire station was built on the site in 1968. It is ironic that it is built on the site of a chip shop as chip pans are one of the major causes of household fires. One fireman from this station, Iain McPhee, was killed while fighting a fire in Lee Bank in 1992, and two others received gallantry medals for their work. The station replaced the one in Albion Street in the Jewellery Quarter. In 1878 there was great excitement when the firemen were able to use their new steam engine for the first time at a fire in a flour mill on Icknield Port Road. In the same year a factory in Freeth Street burned down. It was a match works!

The corner of Friston Street and Ledsam Street. A small advert beneath the 'Surf boils spotless' advert reads 'Vote Conservative' and another reads 'COBB X'. This is partly covered by a Billy Graham advertisement!

Oratory School pupils look at the changing street patterns in Ladywood for a project in 1992. This walkway delineates the route of the former Ledsam Street, which today is truncated at Great Tindal Street. The shops in the picture above were located near here. The pupils are Hayley Worth, Charlotte Dawe, Danielle McIntosh and Elaine Egan.

The Ladywood Road end of Rann Street, January 1961. Rann Street was the birthplace of Sax Rohmer, the creator of Fu Manchu, but he left the area before he was three years old. Rann disappeared as a street name in the 1960s redevelopments and for a while one of the meeting rooms in the Community Centre was called the Rann Room. That too has now disappeared. Mr Rann once lived in Ladywood House on what is now the site of the Methodist church on St Vincent Street. He set up a regiment to fight in the American War of Independence, and this ditty was sung by his troops: 'Heads up, eyes right, we'll stand and fight, Our flag is new and spanky; And Colonel Rann, he is the man to wallop every Yankee.'

Pupils at the Oratory School, under the guidance of teacher Margaret Grew, who was born in Ladywood, and Norman Bartlam, the author of this book, undertook a street naming project as part of a project organised by the award-winning Housing Education Intitiative. Pupils researched the history of the area to come up with suitable names for two new culs-de-sac which were built off Gilby Road. Pupils then put their findings to a panel of local residents and the names were approved. Rann Close was one name chosen, and Power Crescent was the other – in memory of Canon Norman Power. Clare Short, MP for Ladywood, unveiled the first road sign in the company of the pupils who selected the names, together with Margaret Grew, Norman Bartlam and Frank Farrell, the headteacher at the school.

The rear of Court no. 23 on Osler Street, 25 October 1965. This was next door to the rolling mills. The courts next door were Helena Terrace and Rotton Park Terrace, while Victoria Terrace, Disraeli Terrace and Lloyd's Terrace were opposite.

The same location today. This is the newly opened Buddhist Temple at the Pagoda on Osler Street.

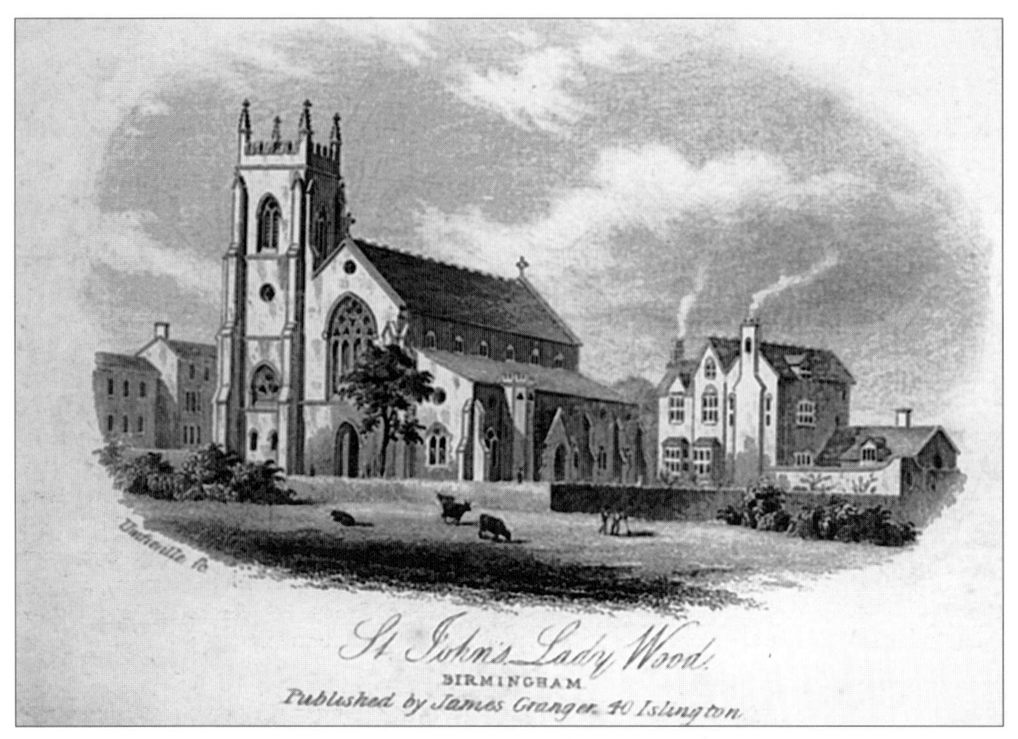

Throughout all the redevelopments St John's Church has remained as a constant reminder of the old Ladywood. This sketch was probably drawn in the 1880s. Cows graze contentedly and the smoke drifts effortlessly from the rather large vicarage. The buildings on the left are on Monument Lane. The publisher of the sketch was based at Islington – which was the name given at the time to Broad Street from Five Ways to Oozells Street.

The church remains in this present-day view, although the vicarage has been rebuilt. The cows have long since moved on and cow horns have been replaced by car horns, for this is the link road from Monument Road to the Ladywood Middleway. On the left stand the offices of the Birmingham Hospital Saturday Fund on Darnley Road. This was founded in 1873 by Joseph Sampson Gamgee, a distinguished surgeon. Workers were invited to work overtime on one Saturday afternoon in the year and donate their earnings to the fund. The modern-day version has over 200,000 subscribers, and benefits include a convalescence home in Weston-super-Mare. Sampson Gamgee lived in a house on the site of the Repertory Theatre.

ACKNOWLEDGEMENTS

Thanks to eveyone who has showed an interest in this book. Particular thanks go to the following for their additional support and advice: Nora Bartlam (née Wilson), Dr Carl Chinn, Jim Cunningham, Myra Curley, Margaret Grew (née Rose), Edie Ockford (née Faulkner), Kathleen Quinlan (née Wilson) and Anthony Spettigue.

Thanks also go to the following people for allowing us to reproduce their pictures or for information that was useful for the captions: Irene Adams (née Parkes), Ernest Bennett, Phil Bowden, Roger Carpenter, Iris Carter (née Wise), Leslie Checkley, Bill Cokayne, Dave Cross of the West Midland Police Museum, Gordon Cull, Denis Daniels, Dave Donovan of the Mint, Sylvia Duffy (née Hunt), Lindy Dunnett (née Carleton), Eileen Doyle, June Felton, Maud Floyd (née Checkley), Darrell Hall of D.T. Hall, Tony Higgs, Kerry, the King Edward's Foundation librarian, Margaret Lee of Lee Longlands, Edward Leigh, Sue Letts of the Co-op, Gareth Lewis, Ernie Link, Ben Lloyd, Mary Martin, Henry Mason, Margaret Miles, Anne Milligan, Don Newport, George Palmer, D.T. Powell, Victor Price, Jack Powell, Angela, Norman Power's daughter, Elsie Rafferty (née Humphries), Ida Russell, David Smith, Sonia Simmonds of PPG Paints, Ken Strangwood, Richard Sykes of Sykes Timber, the Revd Richard Tetlow of St John's Church, Albert Trapp, T.S. Vernon archive, Arthur Unitt, Iris Wise (née Carter) and the people who didn't want to be identified!

The latest new houses in Ladywood are on Sheepcote Street, and are known officially as Symphony Court; or (locally) as 'the posh houses round the corner'! The 147 houses and apartments are built on the triangle of land between the street and the two arms of the canal. Nile Street once ran through the middle of it. These new buildings are part of the Brindleyplace development and were designed in a Dutch architectural style, which fits in well with the canalside setting.

INDEX OF STREET NAMES

Alexandra Street 42, 43
Alston Street 17, 33, 111, 133, 136
Anderton Street 41, 42, 43, 44, 120

Beach Street 26, 28, 29, 109, 134
Beaufort Road 11, 73, 91, 137
Broad Street 10, 13, 49, 51, 55, 64, 66, 121, 146, 147, 148, 150
Browning Street 143

Chamberlain Gardens 17, 128, 129, 137
Clark Street 19, 104, 119, 130
Cope Street 105, 106
Coxwell Road 19, 36, 91, 119

Darnley Road 13, 18, 90, 91, 158
Duchess Road 11, 45
Dudley Road 72

Edward Street 34, 44, 89
Ellen Street 46, 47

Five Ways 13, 135, 139
Freeth Street 21, 27, 28, 59, 61, 80, 81, 82, 104, 110, 152, 154
Friston Street 136, 155

Garbett Street 42, 43, 144
Gilby Road 135, 139, 140, 141, 156
Goodman Street 41
Great Tindal Street 30, 32, 34, 134, 143, 144
Grosvenor Street West 14, 153

Hagley Road 9, 91, 93
Hyde Road 18, 19, 23

Icknield Port Road 21, 22, 23, 39, 58, 59, 60, 68, 72, 87, 91, 104, 106, 130, 152, 154
Icknield Square 25, 27, 29, 59, 63, 94
Icknield Street 48, 62, 97, 112
Ingleby Street 41

Johnstone Street 33, 77, 111

King Edwards Road 41, 43, 45, 107, 149

Ladywood Middleway 28, 126, 133, 134, 135, 137, 138, 139, 153, 158
Ladywood Road 15, 16, 30, 69, 70, 135, 136, 140, 141, 153, 156
Leach Street 25
Ledsam Street 25, 31, 32, 63, 88, 108, 109, 116, 144, 145, 151, 155
Louisa Street 38

Monument Road 10, 12, 13, 16, 17, 22, 24, 25, 26, 28, 31, 41, 45, 52, 72, 84, 85, 86, 88, 92, 96, 102, 106, 129, 133, 134, 158
Morville Street 15, 40, 44, 103, 139

Nelson Street 37, 130

Oliver Road 13, 76, 141
Oozells Street 55, 56, 66
Osler Street 20, 78, 79, 80, 136, 141, 157

Parker Street 16

Rann Street 121, 133, 136, 156
Reservoir Road 20, 104, 122, 123, 124, 125, 126, 141
Rotton Park Street 58, 59, 60, 117
Ruston Street 10, 15
Ryland Street 14, 76

St Marks Street 1, 38, 39, 40, 41, 42, 66, 74, 83, 119
St Mary Street 33, 34, 77, 120
St Vincent Street 30, 31, 37, 50, 126, 131, 136, 138, 143, 156
Shakespeare Road 42, 144
Sheepcote Street/Lane 35, 36, 37, 50, 53, 57, 117, 118, 143, 159
Sherborne Street 30, 103
Spring Hill 41, 46, 47, 48, 49, 89, 102, 112, 127, 139
Stour Street 107
Summerhill 95, 98, 101, 105, 127

Warstone Lane 71
Waterworks Road 8
Wood Street 24, 133, 136, 141
Wyndham Road 93